Social Networking

Make Money Online

BITTU KUMAR

Published by:

F-2/16, Ansari road, Daryaganj, New Delhi-110002
☎ 23240026, 23240027 • *Fax:* 011-23240028
Email: info@vspublishers.com

Branch : Hyderabad
5-1-707/1, Brij Bhawan (Beside Central Bank of India Lane)
Bank Street, Koti, Hyderabad - 500 095
☎ 040-24737290
E-mail: vspublishershyd@gmail.com

Follow us on:

All books available at **www.vspublishers.com**

© **Copyright:** V&S PUBLISHERS
ISBN 978-93-815886-6-6
Edition: 2012

The Copyright of this book, as well as all matter contained herein (including illustrations) rests with the Publishers. No person shall copy the name of the book, its title design, matter and illustrations in any form and in any language, totally or partially or in any distorted form. Anybody doing so shall face legal action and will be responsible for damages.

Printed at: Param Offseters, Okhla, New Delhi-110020

Dedication

*This Book is dedicated to
Nirankari Baba Hardev Singh Ji Maharaj,
who inspired me to do something new,
something innovative.*

Acknowledgements

I would like to express my deepest appreciation to my Parents: they constantly and convincingly conveyed a spirit of adventure in regard to writing. Without their guidance and persistent help this publication would not have been possible.

In addition, a special thanks to V&S Publishers, for giving me the opportunity to develop this book.

I must acknowledge many friends, colleagues, teachers, other artists who assisted, advised, and supported my work and writing efforts over the years. Especially, I need to express my gratitude and deep appreciation to my maternal Uncle Narendra Kumar. Nirankari Mission's hospitality, knowledge, and wisdom have supported, enlightened, and entertained me; they have consistently helped me keep perspective on what is important in life and shown me how to deal with reality.

I am grateful too for the support of my dear friend Mukesh Kumar. I need to thank Maki Starfield (Kyoto, Japan) and many Authors who contributed by giving their personal account snapshots for development of this project.

Thank you once again…

– Bittu Kumar

Contents

Introduction	9
Starting with E-mail	11
Everything about Blogging, First Way of Making Money Online	33
Google AdSense, the way to your Blogging Money	43
Promoting Your Website	49
Affiliate Marketing	63
Social Networking: Money Printing Machine	67
Basic Facebook	75
Facebook Marketing Tools	95
E-Mail Marketing & Newsletters	121
Online Scam, Identity Theft & Prevention	125

Introduction

With Right Mindset, making money becomes a way of life. Even if you are not born with that mindset it can be acquired with a bit of effort. Positive mind with Combined Hard Work help to rake in money. You might have thought that it's easy to think like a millionaire when reading a certain book on topics how to become one. At present you may not have that much money in your bank account, but the state of being millionaire starts in your mind.

One of the most important items needed to the way of wealth is a budget. Not having a budget is like shooting a gun at a target blindfold. So before start reading this book, plan what is your budget and set your goals strictly according to your budget. Make a plan and stick to it and you will see you are doing better… & better.

Now, is it possible to work less and actually make more money?

Yes it is possible.

With 4 billion users and more than 6 billion registered websites the Internet dominates itself as the Principal Marketplace. It provides employment to billions of people and has the capability to generate more than million dollars especially for you…

To become a millionaire in one year you need to earn Rs. 27,898 Per day. And it is very easy to earn this much money with an online hard work for just 15 days.

To start, you will need a computer, little Knowledge of English and active internet connection.

With this reference book, you will not only learn how to become a millionaire but you will also learn about E-mails, Blogging,

Social Networking

how to make your own website, search engine optimization, promoting your website, social networking & E-commerce.

The language and content of this book is user-friendly... designed especially for you, so that you can try it at your own.

If you strictly follow this book for 15 days and use your little portion of brain you will find yourself earning Rs. 27,398 every day and after one year you will be a MILLIONAIRE!

Chapter 1

Starting with E-mail

E-mail is the abbreviated form of Electronic mail; it is the cheapest and fastest means of communication. Sitting in any corner of the world you can receive, send and process E-mails, provided that you have Internet browsing device and your E-mail Id. Don't worry; you need not require purchasing any device right now if you have your PC Ready. Now tighten your seat belts we have started our journey!!!

Here we are featuring Gmail the abbreviated form of Google Mail, the topmost email provider in the world. Once you learn how to use Gmail, you can easily make your E-mail ids on other domains too.

Social Networking

Creating an account

One question a lot of people seem to have is the difference between a Google account and a Gmail account. They are not necessarily the same thing. The catch is, you are allowed to create a Google account using your existing email account. That is not a Gmail account, but an account that allows you access to some of Google's services. One the other hand, if you do create a Gmail account, it automatically becomes your Google account with access to all of Google's services using that id and password. So basically, Gmail accounts are always Google Accounts, but Google Accounts aren't Gmail accounts if you are using a different email from *username@gmail.com*. So then, how do you create a Gmail account?

1. Go to http://www.gmail.com
2. Click the button that says "Create an account" on the bottom right box

New to Gmail? **CREATE AN ACCOUNT**

3. Carefully fill out all the fields on the form
4. Click "I accept. Create my account"

You will be taken to an introduction page. Click "Show me my account". You will be taken to your new email account and there will be some emails from the Gmail Team welcoming you, introducing you to some of the features and helping you import your contacts and old mail.

Starting with E-mail

[Form fields shown: Name (First, Last), Choose your username (@gmail.com), Create a password, Confirm your password, Birthday (Month, Day, Year), Gender (I am...), Mobile phone (+91), Other email address, Prove you're not a robot: "near ecreig", Type the two pieces of text:]

Gmail as a Google Account

So now that you have created a Gmail account, can you use it for anything, be email? The answer is yes. As explained above, Gmail accounts are also Google accounts, and though I were explained all services associated with them, you should know that you can use your Gmail id and password on many Google services, such as:

- ☆ Google Analytics – To track visitors to your website
- ☆ Blogger – Blogging site
- ☆ Google Calendar – A calendar directly integrated with Gmail
- ☆ Google Docs – An online document editor directly integrated with Gmail
- ☆ Microsoft Office online substitute.

Social Networking

- ☆ YouTube – Online video streaming
- ☆ Google Sites – To create websites and wikis
- ☆ Google Dashboard – Your portal to all of the Google services that can be accessed with your Gmail or Google account, from one interface.

And many, many more services and sites.

Gmail's Interface

Though most of Gmail's email functions are similar to the ones you might have used in other email services, it's common to have to take a little time to acquaint yourself to a different interface. Below is a simple guide to using Gmail's web interface:

1 – Inbox

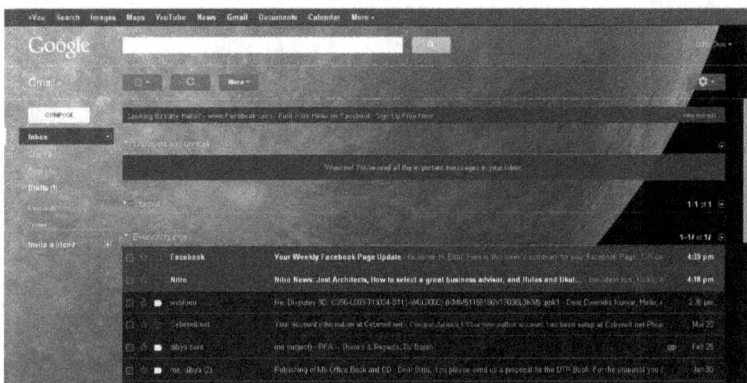

It is where you will find the email you have received and also where you will find replies you have written to those emails. Gmail stacks the messages sent back and forth between 2 or more people so that you can view them all as a single strand, and easily follow conversations up as shown on the example below.

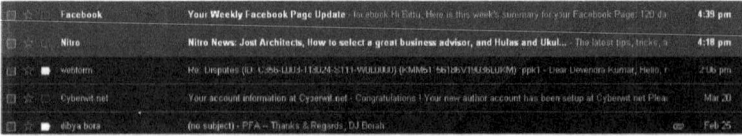

2 – Compose Mail

It is what you would click to start writing an email. You can either type the full email address or start typing the first few letters and Gmail will search through your contact list and give you email address options to choose from. You can also click on the "To" button to be taken to your contact list where you can choose the email you want to use. When writing your email, by putting your mouse over the buttons on the compose panel, you can tell what each button does, be it change colour, font, insert image or link.

3 – Drafts

Gmail will save a copy of the email you are writing as you write it as a "draft". It will do so on small time intervals, but if you decide to save it yourself, you can always just click on the button that says "Save Now" on the bottom of the compose window.

When you do that, a copy gets saved on the Draft folder, so you can continue to write it later if you prefer. Once you send the message, they automatically disappear from the Drafts folder.

4 – Sent Mail

All the email you have ever sent someone can be found by clicking the "Sent Mail" button. It will separate the emails you have sent from the ones sent to you so you can clearly see only the ones you sent yourself.

5– More

The "More" button opens a series of options such as your "Spam" and "Trash". You can drag those labels in and out of the more buttons to customise how you want to view the main buttons on your email, so if you decide you want to have your "Trash" button readily available under the inbox, just drag it there, and if you decide you want your "Drafts" under the "More" button, just drag it there.

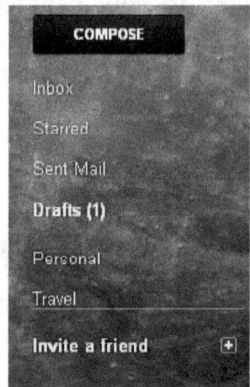
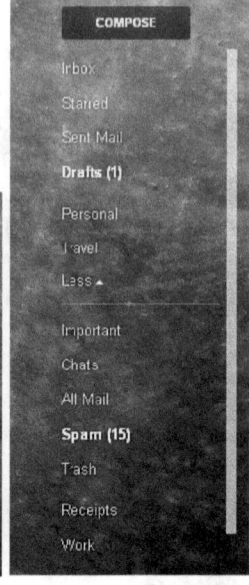

6 – Report Spam

Gmail tends to do a great job keeping spam out of your inbox, but if you do receive some, or there is some insistent company that keeps emailing you even though you asked to be removed from their mailing list, simply select that email and click on "Report Spam". It will make any emails from that address go straight to spam, and it will help Gmail recognise it in the future.

7 – Delete

Because your storage space with Gmail is constantly growing, it is unnecessary, for most people, to ever need to delete emails. If you just don't want to see a certain email on your inbox anymore, check the box next to that email and click the delete button. It will be moved to your trash folder. If you permanently want to remove your email, delete it out of your trash folder as well.

Organising your Gmail

Over time, you may receive thousands of emails, and trying to find a certain email can become a difficult task. That is why

Starting with E-mail

it is important to organise your emails so you can easily find important ones in the future. Below are some useful features to help organise all your emails and contacts.

Contacts

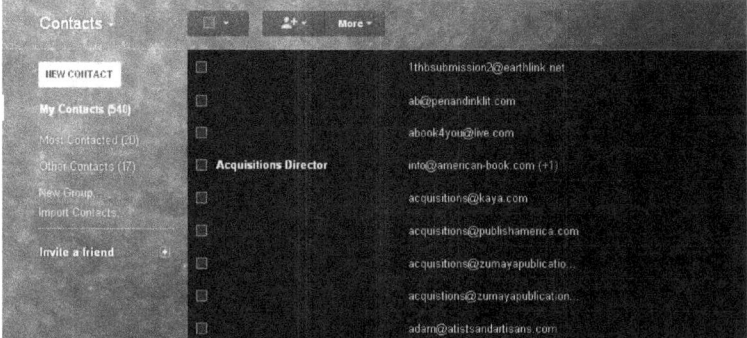

There are several ways to add and organise your contacts. Click on the "Contacts" button on the left hand corner bar and you will be taken to a new page. One very useful thing about Gmail is that you don't really have to add your contacts by hand in the long run. Gmail will automatically add the emails of everyone you replied to or have written to Gmail will, by default, show you initially the most used contacts you have. To view contacts that don't appear on that list, either use the search feature or click on the button that says "All".

By clicking on the single little person with a + sign on the upper left hand side, you can add individual contacts.

By clicking on the multiple little people with a plus sign, also on the upper left hand side, you can create a group. You can move several people to each group, so when you need to email them you don't need to select them one by one. For example, when I am working on a project with a certain number of people, I create a group called "Project Whatever Name" and add to it all the people who are part of that project. That way, when I need to send them all a common email, all I need to do is select that group on the email address field and they will all receive the email. You will notice that Gmail has already created a few groups for you if you decide to use them.

They are the "Friends", "Family" and "Coworkers" groups you see to your left of the screen.

On the upper right hand corner you will notice the import and export buttons. You can import your contacts formatted as CSV files from Outlook, Outlook Express, Yahoo! Mail, Hotmail, Eudora and some other apps. Gmail also supports importing vCard from apps like Apple Address Book.

The Export button is used if you want to do the opposite, export all of your contacts to use in another program or as a back up.

You can also print contact information if you prefer hard copy. Gmail will also help you manage your duplicate contacts by merging them or removing old contacts. You can also click on someone's name and view all your recent conversations you have had, which means, you can see all the emails you exchanged recently. You can also do that simply by searching for the email address or the name of a contact on the search bar on the main screen.

Stars

Stars function in Gmail as a way of marking emails that you would like to pay attention to. You can star an email simply by clicking on the little star icon on the left hand side of any email when on inbox preview. When you decide to look for them again, you can simply click on the 'Starred' button and it will retrieve all the emails you have chosen to mark with a star.

Labels

Labels are a much more elaborate way of organising your emails. They work in a very similar manner to folders in other email clients. You can create labels by clicking on the button on top of the messages that says "Labels" and selecting "Manage Labels". You will then be taken to a page that lets you manage all of your labels, whether you want to show them or hide them from the left side menu, and the option to delete them or create new ones.

Starting with E-mail

When you decide to add an email to a particular label, simply check the box next to that email, go to the label pull down and check the label you want to be assigned to that email. Much like the stars, or folders, if at point you want to view only emails that have that label, click on the name of the label on the left hand side menu and all the emails you have attached that label to will appear.

You can also "mute" an email. Let's say you signed up for a mailing list, you want to receive, so they are not spam, but they send emails so frequently that you don't want to see it popping up all the time. Well, you can go to "more actions" and select "Mute" or simply type the letter "m" when reading one of the emails, and from then on, all emails coming from that group will bypass the inbox and go directly to archive, where you can find them when you do want to read the message.

Advanced Settings

There are many settings to choose from with Gmail. Some control basic features, some add features to the emails, some determine how you reply, who you receive emails from, and how you use your Gmail services. Below is a brief guideline for some of those settings. You can Access them by clicking on the "Settings" button on the upper left hand corner of your Gmail window.

Social Networking

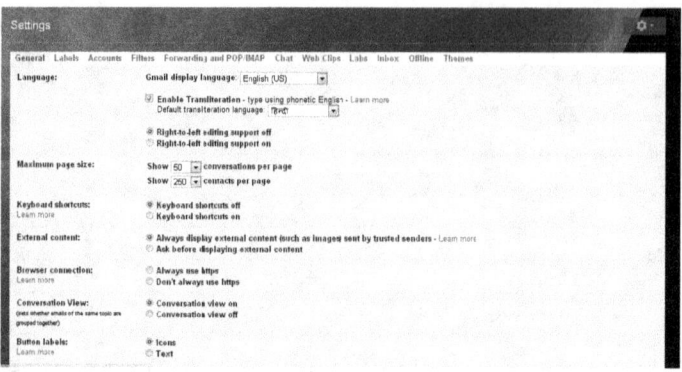

General Settings

There are many things you can determine from the general settings. A few examples are:

1. Maximum Page size: It determines how many emails you see at a time (the default is 50). Just remember, making that number very large can make your page load slower.
2. My Pictures: It allows you to upload a picture which will be seen by your friends when they chat with you, move their mouse over your name on the chat bar, on Buzz, or throughout your Gmail pages. It's a great way to personalise Gmail. There is also a setting to determine whether you get to see the picturesyour friends uploaded.
3. Signature: You can write something inside the box that would appear on the bottom of every email you write. Some people use that to add their contact information without having to type it every time. Others use it to add something fun, like a quote or a saying they like.
4. Vacation Responder: Let's you add a message that will automatically be sent to anyone who emails you during a certain period of time. That way if some business email comes in, you can add the auto responder to reply with an alternate contact while you are away and a message saying when you are coming back. It is also useful for

friends who might not realise you are away and who will be wondering why you aren't replying to their emails.

Accounts and Import

It is under these settings that Gmail has options to help you import your email and contacts from other email accounts. Simply click the button that says import mail and contacts and follow the prompts. It will ask for your email and password and email will attempt to import all of the information. In certain cases, such as when you are trying to import emails from your personal website, you might have to add information, such as pop server.

You can also use Gmail as a substitute to use your own URL email, such as yourname@yourwebsite.com, without people realising you are doing it. That's where the "Send mail as" can be handy. The easiest way to make use of this is to set whatever your other email is to forward to your Gmail account. From that point, click on the "Send mail another address" button. Enter your name and the other email address and click next step. Gmail will send that email a confirmation number that you have to type in that box to prove that you are the person receiving that email. One you have added that number, you can select to either make that email your default responder, or it will be one of the emails on a pull down you can select to respond as. You can also have Google host the email for your domain, by using Google Apps, that way you would use your own domain address but within the Gmail interface.

To sign up to Google Apps, visit http://www.google.com/a

Check mail using Pop3 allows you to import emails from different accounts, so you can read them and reply to them via Gmail. Gmail allows you to do that to as many as 5 email addresses. The difference between that and the forwarding option is that this allows you to get those emails on Gmail while still receiving them on your original email address.

Filters

The Filter setting allows you to manage spam and choose how to handle certain messages. Click on "Create new filter" and you can decide to "filter" a certain email address, subject and even specific words. You can then decide how you want that filter to be applied. The options include:

- ★ Skip the Inbox (Archive it)
- ★ Mark as read
- ★ Star it
- ★ Apply the label
- ★ Forward it to
- ★ Delete it
- ★ Never send it to Spam

Forwarding and Pop/IMAP

What happens if you have a favourite email client, such as Outlook or Thunderbird, but you still want to use Gmail? You can control your options to either forward Gmail emails to another email address, or to set it up to work with other email clients so you can download your email to view on your computer or as a way of archiving the email in a physical location as opposed to on the Google cloud.

Offline

Another great feature is the ability to have access to your Gmail even when you are not online. So let's say you are on a plane with no web access, but it is also the perfect opportunity to catch up with all of those emails you haven't had a chance to reply to. If you enable Gmail offline, it will download the email to your computer, so that you can reply to and read your email, or catch up on adding contacts and when you go back online, those messages will be sent and Gmail will catch up to everything you did while offline. You can even add attachments that will be sent when you are back online.

It even has a "flaky connection mode" which helps Gmail adjust to the internet connection you have if it is unreliable and download the messages to your computer as the connection comes and goes. That way, you don't have to worry that you will lose the emails you have typed if you suddenly go offline. Gmail will catch itself up to the changes you made offline when the computer goes back online.

To turn offline on, click on the "create a desktop shortcut" and Gmail will create an icon on your desktop to make it easier for you to access it while offline. It's almost like having an email program installed on your computer but with the Gmail features and with the knowledge that if your computer breaks, you still have all of your emails and contacts safely stored with Google.

The Fun Stuff

Gmail is not just about work though. The folks at Google have added a few features to ensure we can also have some fun while emailing. To access any of the settings for the features below, click on "Settings" on the upper right hand corner of your email.

Buzz

Buzz is basically Gmail's response to Facebook and Twitter. It is meant to work as a social network that you opt into if you want to use it. It is not active on your account by default. You can follow people on your email list and be followed, see their status updates and post pictures and video to share with each other. You can also use it to import your stuff from Twitter, Picasa, Flickr, and Google Reader. And share them with your friends and contacts.

Buzz can be enabled and disabled by going to "Settings > Buzz". You can choose to show it on Gmail, whether to make your Buzz contact lists public, or whether to enable or disable it completely.

Chat

The chat is a quick way to communicate with friends when emailing doesn't seem to be the best way to do it and you only need some quick and instant back and forth. It can only be used

Social Networking

between Gmail users and even then, only between those who have accepted and opted in to accept chats, but that is still a surprisingly large number of Gmail users. All you have to do to chat with someone is look for their name on the chat box on the left hand side of the screen. Check if they are online, which you can tell by looking for a small green dot next to their name. Double click on their name and a little chat window will appear. Start typing your message and click send (or enter). They will hear a little warning and a small window will appear that allows them to read your message and type back. In case they log off while you are typing, you will be told they are now offline and be given an option to send the chat as an email instead, which they will receive when they get back online. You can also sign into AIM by using the same interface and chat with your AIM friends as well.

Web Clips

When Gmail was just launched, there were certain concerns that Gmail would be mining information from the emails to post ads that were relevant to you. The truth is that there is an algorithm that determines what ads would be most relevant depending on key words from the emails, but no private information is ever sent to Google. Another way to control what you see on top of your inbox and related ads is by using "Web Clips", which can be found under "Settings >Webclips". It is basically a way to control what you want to see displayed above your inbox. You can choose among hundreds of feeds, custom content from major sites such as CNN, Forbes, YouTube, news and yes, even ads. And if you prefer, you can even disable them all together.

Labs

Labs adds a whole new dimension to your email experience, which makes you an active participant on the development of your email features. What Google has created with Labs, is a way of testing features they are considering implementing on their email, as well as trying some of the totally wacky, but sometimes surprisingly useful add-ons Google created for their email.

Because many of those features are being tested, some of the features come and go, but they are certainly worth a try anyway.

Themes

Now, for some people, the Gmail look is dull and boring. Fear not… If the standard Gmail interface is too tame for you, Google has thought of people just like you and added "Themes" to Gmail. Basically it allows you to choose from several looks.

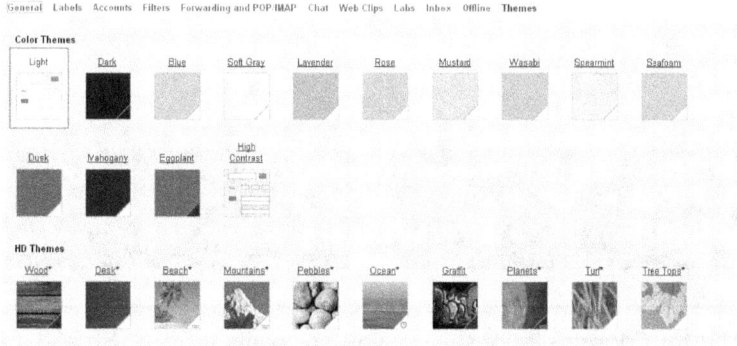

Gmail Mobile

There are many ways to integrate Gmail into your phone, be it an Android phone, another smartphone or a simple Java capable phone. You can download a simple bookmark to connect you to the mobile version of Gmail by going to http://www.google.com.au/mobile/mail/. From that page you can even have Google send you the link to your phone via text message. Android and smartphones have a plethora of options to choose phone be it integrating the email with their phone, importing the email into the email program, or simply accessing it online. Gmail was built to be easily accessible by people on the move.

From any phone, you can go to http://gmail.com to get the Gmail web app or access the mobile version of Gmail.

Social Networking

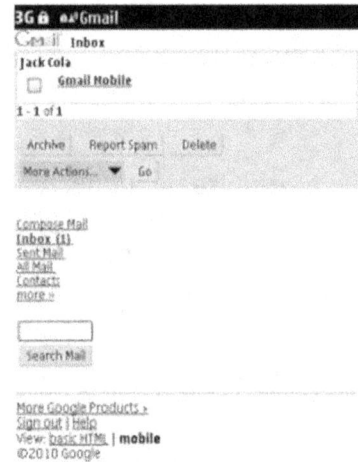 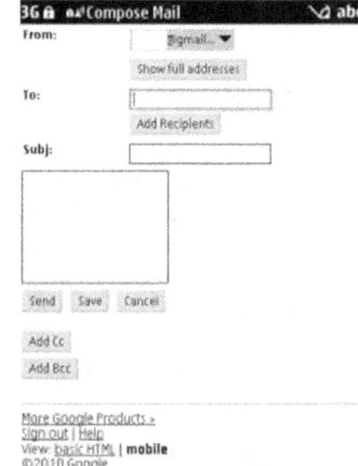

> **Note:** Congratulations! Now you are really a Gmail Expert! If you have practiced well, and can manage your Gmail Id you can now tighten your seat belt for next level, you still believe you need to learn more, go back and practice more and more… And I believe you will become ready for the next level.
>
> **Tip:** Make Gmail accounts for your family and manage them for a while.

☆ Hurrah! Now next time you need not ask what E-mail or Gmail is! You are doing well, keep going ahead like this and you will be surely a Millionaire.

A Powerful Payment Tool – PayPal

Before learning how to earn more money online, you need to learn what PayPal is. This will be your friend to send your online earnings in your Bank Account.

Please be careful and concentrate while reading this section.

Introduction

Account holders traditionally create PayPal accounts by going directly to PayPal.com or signing up during a checkout flow. The Adaptive Accounts CreateAccount method offers a new way – Creating accounts within your application or website, outside the checkout flow.

Your application sends a request using the CreateAccount method with information gathered from your application user's website, and PayPal creates the account. At that point, the new PayPal account holder is briefly redirected to PayPal.com to enter private information, such as a password and to accept the PayPal User Agreement. Your application then returns Adding Bank.

Accounts as Funding Sources

In addition to creating and verifying PayPal accounts, Adaptive Accounts lets your application link bank accounts to PayPal accounts as funding sources. Traditionally, PayPal account holders do this manually at PayPal.com. With the AddBankAccount method, you can now offer your customers the benefit of a smooth, uninterrupted process where PayPal account creation includes adding a funding source for the account, all in one fell swoop. If you are a financial institution, you can offer customers who are also PayPal account holders an easy way to link the bank account with your institution as a funding source for their PayPal accounts. How does it work? Your application sends an AddBankAccount request, passing the relevant bank account information, such as the account number and routing number. The PayPal account holder is redirected briefly to PayPal.com to confirm the information, then returns to your customer's website.

Adding Payment Cards as Funding Sources

Adaptive Accounts lets your application link the created PayPal account to a credit card or payment card. This card can then be used as a funding source (payment method) for the PayPal account. To use this feature, you use the createAccount key from the CreateAccount response and pass it with the AddPaymentCard method together with pertinent payment card information.

Social Networking

For standard permissions, the AddPaymentCard method requires the PayPal account user to confirm the payment card addition on paypal.com. Developers with advanced permissions can pass the AddPayment Card with the confirmed Type element (set to NONE) to add payment cards without redirecting to PayPal.com.

Supported payment cards are:
- Visa
- MasterCard
- American Express
- Discover
- Maestro
- Solo
- Carte Aurore
- Carte Bleue
- Cofinoga
- 4 Etoiles
- Carte Aura
- Tarjeta Aurora
- JCB

Set Funding Sources to Confirmed Status

If you call the AddBankAccount or AddPaymentCard methods, you can use the SetFundingSourceConfirmed method to set the created funding source to "confirmed". In certain instances, this will cause the PayPal account status to be set to Verified.

Confirming PayPal Verified Status

A huge challenge that merchants face today is fraud. The GetVerifiedStatus method is a great way to help PayPal merchants reduce the loss of precious profits through fraud. It works like this: Before your customer (a PayPal merchant) engages in a transaction, your application sends a GetVerifiedStatus request. This request contains specific criteria you want to match, such as the PayPal account holder's email address. The Adaptive Accounts

Starting with E-mail

web service responds with a message that indicates if the match was verified. This lets you offer your customers a powerful tool for reducing fraud. With the GetVerifiedStatus method, merchants have the security of knowing that consumers' PayPal accounts are verified before completing a transaction. This can be of great value for large transactions.

Creating PayPal account:

To create PayPal account you need to login to www.paypal.com/login, a form will appear as shown in the screen. Fill the fields with required data and Click on yellow button that says "I Agree Create My Account".

Note – *Indian Customers can be asked here to give their PAN card details or TIN/CIN details. Please do not supply junk data, it will result in deactivation. The Information is checked and verified by experts.*

The Next Screen will ask for your Credit Card & Debit Card Details; you can add as well as cancel to add the information. But adding these data now will help saving your time in future.

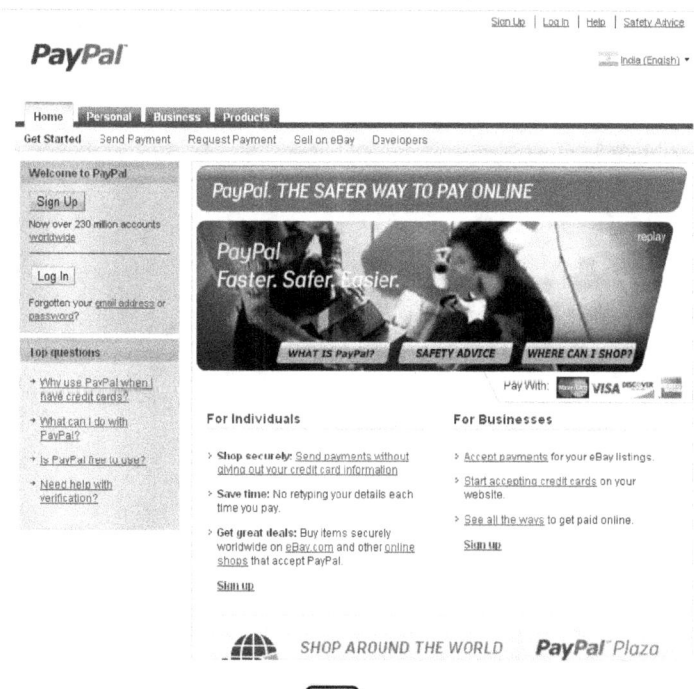

Social Networking

PayPal

Create your PayPal account Secure

Your country or region
India

Already have a PayPal account? Upgrade now.

Personal
An account for online shoppers to make payments

- Free to sign up and buy.

[Get Started]

Premier
An account for casual sellers who occasionally buy online

- Free to sign up and buy.
- Low fees charged for receiving payments.

[Get Started]

Business
For merchants with a company or group name and high transaction volumes

- Free to sign up. Low fees charged for receiving payments.
- You can accept all payment types for low fees.

[Get Started]

Learn more about PayPal account types.

PayPal

Enter your information

(Form fields: Email address, Choose a password, Re-enter password, First name, Middle name, Last name, Date of birth, Nationality, Business PAN, Address line 1, Address line 2, Town/City, State, PIN code, Mobile Number)

[Agree and Create Account]

Contact Us

Starting with E-mail

If you want to add cards fill the fields and provide your genuine billing and shipping address. You can simply then click orange "Add Card" button to proceed. To cancel, you can use grey "cancel" button.

You will see the following screen after clicking on any of these buttons confirming your login successful.

Now you are ready with your personal PayPal account.

Note – *Indian customers will go a PAN/TIN/CIN verification and Bank account verification too. You will receive two small payments in your Bank account within two days after adding your Bank account. Verify your bank account to the server by inserting the amount of payments you received.*

Merchant Referral Program Bonus

These days you can use PayPal for Generating Online Income; through The Merchant Referral program.

Social Networking

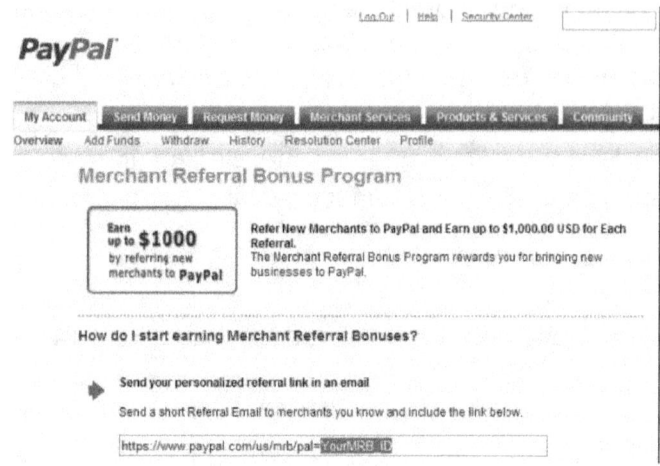

On signing up for PayPal you will get your Unique Referral Link as shown in diagram. Send this link to your Network. More the Number of Persons join with this link more will be your Referral Bonus.

So what are you waiting for?

Since we are preparing to become a Millionaire, we need to receive payments. After the login, you will get a unique PayPal ID, but your PayPal Id will be similar to your Email Id, so next time whenever you sign up for AdSense or Any other Affiliate program (you will learn about it later) just select to get payment from PayPal and Relax! Your money making plant will grow without any problem.

> **Tipoff**
> Now you know the basics flow of money on Internet. Now the time for some exercises. To practice PayPal, at least help 5 persons getting online payment via PayPal. And you will become an expert in PayPal Application.
>
> Never Provide junk data on PayPal. This is a punishable offence.
>
> ☆ Legal Note: Neither the Publisher nor the Author has affiliation with PayPal.

Chapter 2

Everything about Blogging, First Way of Making Money Online

Focus on this chapter; in this chapter you will learn the first way to Earn Genuine Money Online!

Creating your own Blog

Step 1: Go To Blogger.com

Blogger is a service provided by Google. Since we have already made our Gmail Id, it will be convenient for us to use Blogger.

Put the following URL on your browser: http://www.blogger.com

The following Screen will appear:

Social Networking

Click on the Orange arrow that says "Create Your Blog Now".

Step 2: Create an Account

For this step, you need to create your Username and Password. It does not matter which Username you use.

You will be asked what display name you want to use; this name will appear in the End of every Blog you write.

Finally select the Email address you made earlier, check the area that says "You agree Their Terms of Service and Agreement."

Once you have entered the information, click on Orange "Continue" Arrow.

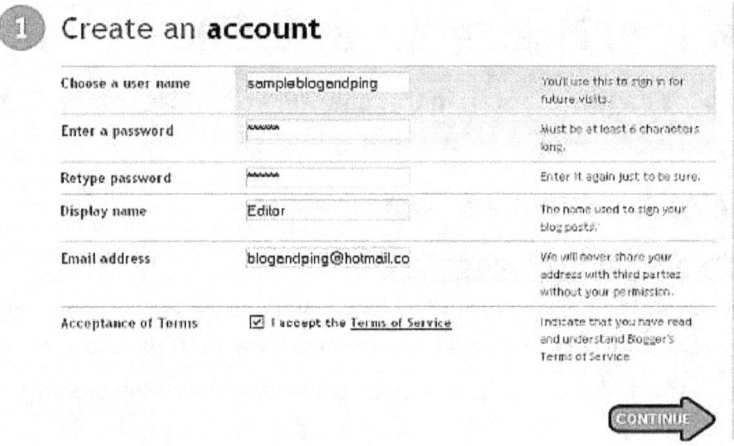

Step 3: Naming your Blog

In the first tab choose a title for your blog, followed by the Blog URL you want. Enter the words you see in image in the Third Tab and again click on the Orange "Continue" arrow.

Sometimes Following Screen may appear when the Entered URL is already in use, don't worry and simply change the URL. Once you are done with URL you can now move to step 4.

Step 4: Choosing a template

Blogger has currently 12 ready-made templates to choose from. Choose one you like from. In the following screen "Son of Motto" has been chosen.

Social Networking

Once again click on the Orange "Continue" arrow.

If you have done everything in the right manner the following screen should appear and you will be notified that your blog has been created. Simply click on the orange arrow that says "Start Posting".

Step 5: Create a Post

In the Tab 'Title' add the Title of your choice. Followed by URL if your post is imported from somewhere, don't be afraid if you don't know the URL, simply leave this field blank. In the third tab write your Subject Matter you use to do in Word files. In the header of the third tab you can observe different signs, you can use them to edit the texts, change the fonts and add Images.

Click on Blue Button that says "Save as Draft" if you want to save it. Click on the Orange Button that says "Publish Post" if you need to publish your post. This screen will appear once you click the Orange Button:

If you click "View Blog" you will be redirected to your blog and it will appear like this:

Now your Blog is successfully created!!!

Now you need to customise some important settings you need for your blog.

Social Networking

For this click on 'Settings' tab, and the following window will appear.

Step 6: Customising settings

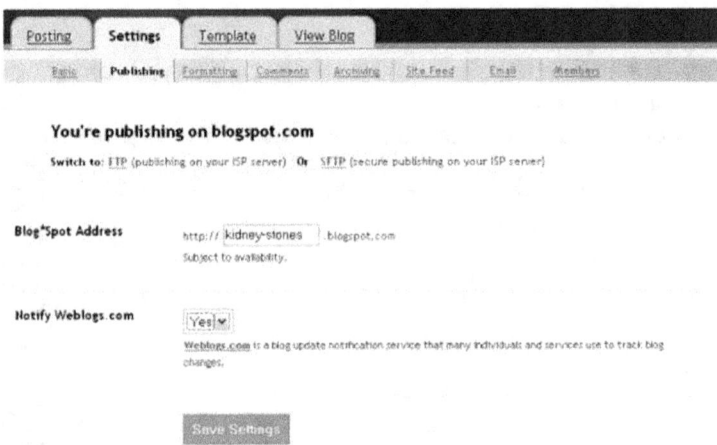

You can edit your Blog's URL and choose to select notification enabled to weblogs.com, after changing the fields, simply click on the orange "Save Settings" button. The following screen will appear:

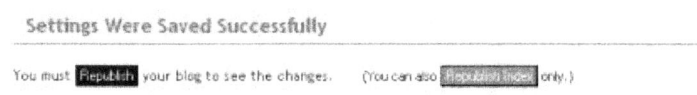

There is no requirement for Republishing your Blog at this time. Next Click on Formatting Tab and the following window will appear.

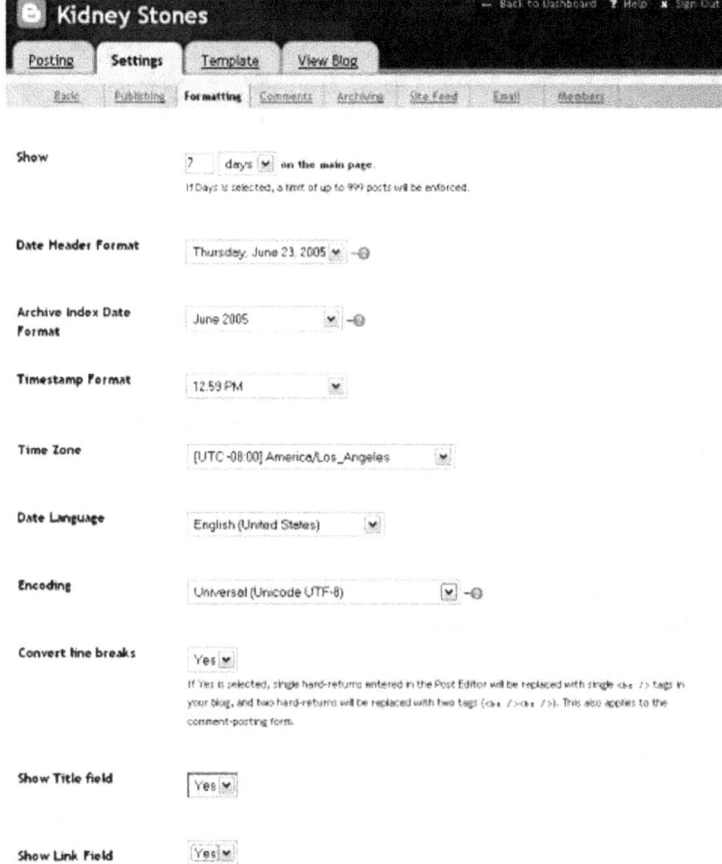

Change the Settings in different tabs according to your need and then Click on the Next Tab "Comment".

The following screen will appear on clicking the tab "Comment":

Social Networking

To allow posts on your blog you will need to make some changes.

"Who can comment" needs to be anyone.

"Comment Notification Area" needs to have a valid e-mail address where you will receive notification of comments and posts to your blog. The following screen will appear:

Make necessary changes and click on Orange "Save Settings" Button.

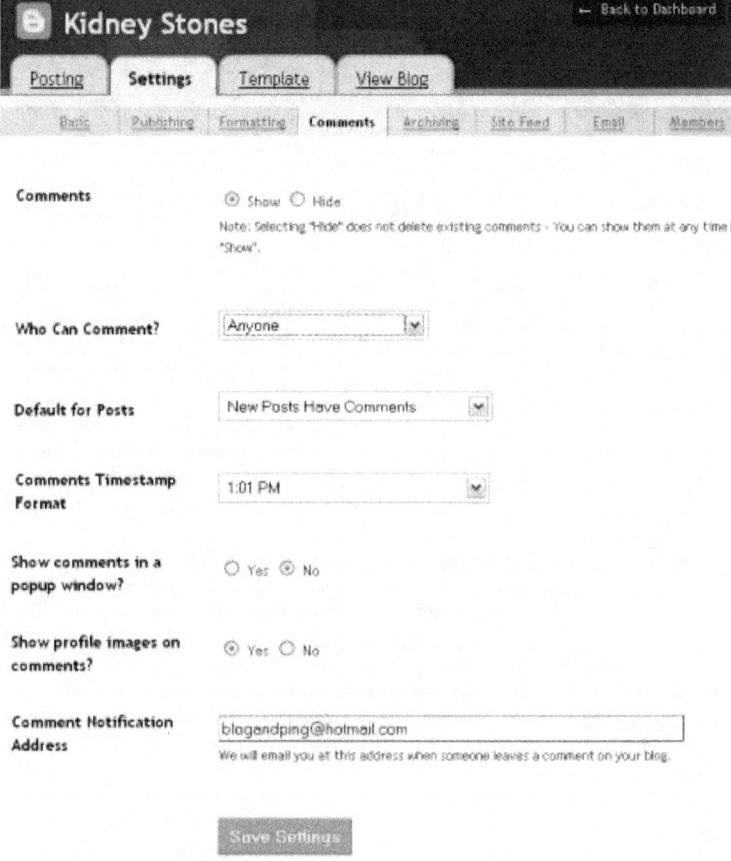

If you want daily archiving of your blog, click the tab Archiving and then change the preset fields. And then again click on the Orange button to save Settings.

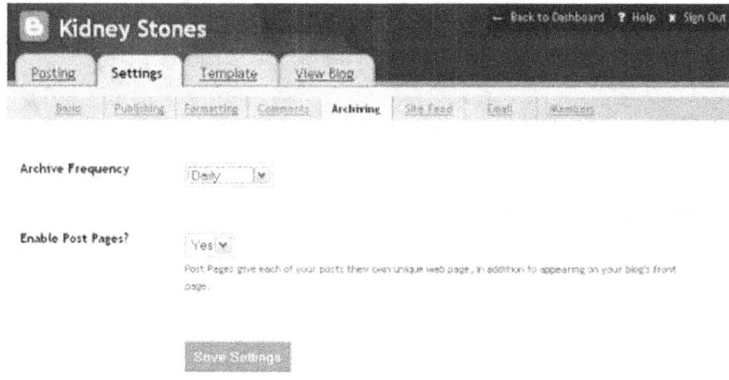

Next come the Site Feed Tab. Click on this tab to check all the settings in these tab are correct

You need not change the fields, just click on the orange button that says "Savesettings".

Step 7: Republish

Republish your Blog so that changes can apply to your blog. And then view your Blog.

Social Networking

Now your Blog is ready... Make more blogs like this to maximise your chances of earning more. (Though I have not yet added how to make money online using blogs, you will learn it next chapter.) Earn millions with your blogs

> **Tipoff**
> I think now you are an expert of blogs. I am analysing that you are doing better and better... If you feel you need more practice, go back and read carefully and practice thoroughly and you will become an expert soon.
>
> Since we need to make Rs. 27398 in one day in initial phase only one blog is unable to contribute this much amount of money. You should at least make 10 similar blogs on different topics.

Chapter 3

Google AdSense, the way to your Blogging Money

I now think you have setup your blog accounts and now you are wondering how you will make money online. This chapter introduces AdSense, a service from Google Inc. And you may not believe a fact that yearly by using this service people earn more than $20 billion yearly in India only!!!

So concentrate on this section and you will find Google AdSense as a Money Yielding plant!

Introduction

In recent years, there has been a great deal of discussion and information concerning Google's AdSense program at http://www.google.com/AdSense.

First, let's take a look at exactly what AdSense is and what it is all about:

"AdSense is a program for webmasters which was implemented by Google some years ago."

Essentially, a webmaster (a person who owns and builds one or more websites) signs up for an account with the program, and once they are approved, they paste the Google AdSense Javascript code into the pages on their websites.

Google then starts serving ads to those websites, based on the keywords that it finds in the text of the page. When a visitor clicks on one of those ads, the webmaster makes money – usually a few cents per click.

However, when a site has a great deal of traffic, and when the webmaster knows which keywords are the most profitable to target, there is a chance of making huge money.

It sounds simple enough, but it's really NOT that easy. First of all, you have to be approved and Google is picky these days. The good news is that once one site is approved, and you have a Google AdSense account, there is no need to seek Google's approval to use AdSense on any other site that you own, as long as that site is within the Google's terms of service guidelines.

Once you are approved, you have to know which keywords to target – the ones that will help you make most amount of money per click, and how to write (or have written for you) content that makes those high paying ads appear on your site.

Finally, you have to learn how to drive traffic to your AdSense site. Without the traffic, you won't get any clicks, and without clicks, you won't be making any money. Getting real, targeted visitors that are eager to click on your ads is by far the hardest part of being an AdSense publisher.

Applying For Your AdSense Account

Once you are prepared to apply for a Google AdSense account, it's as simple as filling out a form. But there are some aspects of that form that can be a bit confusing.

In this section, I'll go over filling out the form, so that Google will approve you without any problems. You can find the form to apply for an AdSense account at:

http://www.google.com/AdSense/g-app-single-1.

The first thing that the form asks for is the URL of your website. Note that even if you have multiple sites, Google only wants to see one. So, list the URL of the site that you have set up for the purpose of being approved for Google AdSense, and enter the URL like this: www.yourdomain.com, or the one you made for your blog.

You do not have to include the http:// part of the URL, and don't include any subpages of the URL, such as www.mydomain.com/mypage.html. Google wants to see the main page of the site, at the top level domain. Next, Google wants to know what language your site is published in. If your site supports multiple languages, this is fine, but this isn't what Google wants to know. They want to know the primary language of the site – this would be the language that you used to write the pages, such as English.

The next question on the form throws a lot of people into a tailspin. It asks if you are setting up an individual or business account. Here is a way to simplify this question: If you do not have an office or business that currently has 20 or more employees, you are an individual. It doesn't matter what your future plans are. Next, select the country that you live in. The following part of the form asks for your personal information: name, street address, city, and state. It is important to note that when Google pays you, the check will be made out to the name that you put here, and sent to the address that you put here. So, use the information that you need to use here in order to receive the check, and to cash or deposit the check. After your name and address, Google wants your telephone number. They probably won't call you, but sometimes they will, if there is a problem or a question. Give that phone number where you can be reached. You do not have to provide a fax number. Here, you can also choose to receive Google's newsletter – or not. Choosing not to receive the newsletter will not have any effect on whether or not you are Approved.

Following this, there are a number of check boxes, all of which must be checked, before you can submit the application. By checking these boxes, you are saying that you will not click on the ads on your pages that you will not encourage visitors to click on your ads (incentives) that you are able to receive checks that are made out to you, that you will not place ads on pornographic sites, and that you have read the AdSense program policies.

Finally, you submit the form, and prepare to wait. Your site will be checked by a live human being. Approval is manual, not automated, and it can take up to three business days (72 hours) before you hear from a Google representative. That contact usually comes via email.

– Wait, what is this "Product selection"?

This appears on the some application form and seems confusing to many – choose both: AdSense for Content and AdSense for Search. This means that you can run both, but don't have to run both.

You can have Google ads appear on your pages (AdSense for Content) and you can also include a Google search box on your pages (AdSense for Search), and when people use those search boxes, and click on sponsored ads in the results, you get paid for those clicks as well.

I Have My Account – Now What?

Congratulations!

Now that you've been approved for a Google Account, by building a site that Google would easily approve, and you've selected a high paying topic for yoursite, you are ready to get to work and build your first profitable AdSense website.

If you have not already done so (you should have), you really need to go and read the program policies that Google has set, as well as their Webmaster Guidelines. This will help you to build a better site, and to avoid issues that can and will get you banned from the Google AdSense program.

You should use all of the search engine optimisation techniques as possible when building your site. (You will learn later in this book about how to make websites. Now you will only place ads on your blogs) Not only will this attract the right ads, but it will also help your site to move up in the search results, for the purpose of driving traffic to your site.

Now, you are ready to place the AdSense javascript code on your pages. Log in to your AdSense account. Click on the AdSense Set up tab at the top of the page.

First, click on Channels, and set up a Channel for the topic of your site. This will come in handy later on, when you are analysing which of your sites is pulling in the most money.

Next, click on Palettes, and create a colour palette that matches your site well. You want your Google ads to blend into your site. If they stand out like a sore thumb, they will get fewer clicks, simply because people really do try to avoid advertisements. You want the ads to look like content on your site. Once you've set up a palette that matches your site, click on products. Choose AdSense for content to create your ad units. Here, you can choose ads that are enclosed in a box, or ads that are more free standing, but still just text links. It is a good idea to choose the link unit to add above or below your navigational links, and you can design your site navigation links to look just like the Google link units.

You should customise your blog to look like this:

Social Networking

Please Note: You need to hire a webmaster for enabling you to use AdSense, since it requires the knowledge of some basic HTML. Please hire a webmaster to activate AdSense on your Blogs. It will cost you only a few hundreds, or sometime free.

Making Traffic on AdSense

You will need traffic on your websites to make much from your AdSense account. For this you will need to connect on Social Networking. Please refer to the Social Networking Section in this Book.

> **Tipoff**
>
> With the help of a webmaster please setup your Google AdSense account on your blogs, and you will find earning yourself some thousand rupees every day.
>
> Now you need to learn more since blogs cannot contribute for Rs.27938 per day in your pocket, and in coming chapters you will find more ways to earn online.
>
> Don't pay too much to your webmaster for doing this little job.

Chapter 4

Promoting Your Website

Four Reasons Why You Need a Website:
Small businesses need internet presence more than large businesses. Why? Here are four reasons
1. **To exist for prospects:** A vast majority of consumers go to the internet when looking for a product or service. If your company is not found, then you do not exist for them. With internet presence you will be able to magnetise multitudes to your unique products and services.
2. **Name recognition:** If consumers don't know about you, because you are a small business, they won't know to type your website address when looking for your service. For example, someone wanting to buy a computer is likely to type in Dell or Apple on the search engines because those names are familiar and recognisable. This is what is meant by name recognition. However, someone looking for a transcription service is unlikely to type gmrtranscription.com (a small transcription company). It is vital, then, that the owners of gmrtranscription.com find internet presence on the search engines. Search engines are vehicles that scan the web searching for a website that matches the key words given it.
3. **To establish credibility and reputation:** Consumers like to research a company over the web before setting a foot in the door. If you do not have internet presence,

you lose them. Large businesses have no such problem because of their better name recognition, reputation and track record.

4. **To widen your sphere of influence:** Large businesses have distribution networks that give them regional, national, or global presence. Internet presence is the first, best and sometimes the only option for small businesses to get national or global presence.

What Is Internet Presence? Of What Does It Consist?

Internet presence does not only mean a website for your business; it also means that when your prospects are looking for the product and services you offer, they find your website. A percentage of those who find your website through a search engine are likely to become your customers if your website is clear, commanding, and creative and meets the criteria in this book.

The good news is that you can quickly compete with your larger competitors through a well-planned and well-executed internet strategy. Moreover, the cost of execution should not be high if you, as a small business owner use creative internet presence options available through website design/marketing companies.

Make sure that your website is an extension of your overall marketing and positioning strategy. Your website design and message should reflect your business philosophy and your unique value proposition (UVP). (USP, unique selling proposition is interchangeable with UVP and is just another way of expressing why people choose your company andproducts/services over other companies with similar products/services.) It is very important to identify why your customers choose you over other people; all things being equal. You might need to survey them to find out, but it any case, it takes careful observation. The main point here is that your marketing strategies must all be integrated and going towards the same direction, all thrusting forward on your purposes towards well defined goals.

Basic Website Usage Facts:

Consumers now use the internet to research providers or products/services and to do background searches of companies before setting foot into the physical location of the business. Make your website a one-stop shop for finding out information about all aspects of your company and the products/services you offer.

Consumers SCAN website pages, they DO NOT READ them. With the exception of sites that provide stories and articles, consumers generally skim the web pages; they do not read the contents word by word. While there may be several reasons for scanning vs. reading, it is a fact and website pages need to be designed for scanning. Some suggestions for pages designed for scanning are:

- ★ Promise the reader something in your page title, tell the reader what to expect from your website. Confirm the promise given by your title in your page description. Educate the customer in the body of the pages by using catchy words and bullet points that are bolded. Invite or call the reader to obvious action.

- ★ Give consumers a satisfactory solution that is easy to find and understand. Contrary to common belief, consumers generally stop at a satisfactory solution rather than compare and get the best solution. They stop when they find something they think will work rather than go on looking for the site that gives them the ideal. This means that you should focus on offering what the page promises in the page title, making the site user friendly, and inviting very clear calls to action. These things will result in the most effective website. The chances of losing a customer because he/she is confused on your site are much higher than losing one because other sites offer a better value. Having said that, the price needs to be within the spectrum of what consumers expect to pay for your products/services.

- ★ Give consumers what they are looking for on your site rather than make them read instructions on "how to use."

Many readers seem to be allergic to reading instructions on how to use something. For example, I'm sure you've heard people say, "I can't stand to read the manual, I'd rather just call tech support or have someone show me how to do it." There is a tendency for people to want to just start using whatever it is they want to use. So, because human nature tends this way, the chances of someone leaving your site because they could not find what they want are significantly higher; even if you have detailed instructions on the site. Thus a site that is easy to use would result in visitors remaining on your site rather than going on to the next one. Website design that follows the "current" layout and provides a site map would prevent visitors from defecting to another site. (A Site Map is a dedicated web page that lists all web pages in a website. This helps a visitor quickly find contents of a website quickly.)

Three Website Challenges for Small Businesses

Is your website not generating the results you want? Are you looking to design a website for your business, or redesign your existing website because it is not generating leads and sales? If so, here are the three obstacles that you need to overcome so that you can start generating your share of the internet revenue from the website:

1. Designing the website – while fairly complex, is the easiest hurdle to jump over.
2. Getting visitors to the website – presents a much higher series of hurdles to overcome than getting a website designed.
3. Converting visitors to customers – is the most complex obstacle course to navigate. Now we're talking about all the realities of business; competition, communication, closing and credibility.

All three challenges are intertwined in the sense that there are many common elements of a website that impact design, visits and conversion. The key is to plan the site upfront. Remember that old graphic on the subject?

PLAN AHEAD

Small Businesses can overcome these three challenges with a well-defined and executed strategy before even starting the website design. The key is planning – knowing what you want the website to do for you before the first code for the website is written.

Store Layout Format: Always look at your website as your store/office and make sure that it follows the basic layout of your store/office. For example, if your website is to follow a store layout, it needs to:

- ✯ Identify your business with a name that reflects what you offer (either a brand that people know or a name that identifies your business – Ex. Paolo's Pizzeria identifies your restaurant as a Pizza shop. Domino's conveys the same thing because it is an established brand).

- ✯ Offer what the name of the store suggests immediately when the site visitor enters your store. Walking in the store (site visit) should instantly confirm that you offer what the name of the store suggests. You can accomplish this result on your website through appropriate page design and its title/description.

- ✯ Use tabs and other visual aids to guide a visitor to items. These visual aids help store visitors find items by following signs for the item or category.

- ✯ Sell products using a shopping cart. Here they will see details of the items repeated such as price, description, postage and time and means of delivery. Of course you have already provided this relevant information in your website.

The following pages provide the seven simple steps to complete an internet strategy of your business. However, please be aware that you need to have a complete strategy in place upfront because the three challenges are connected to each other.

STEP I: Preparation

To repeat this principle; your strategy to get effective internet presence must be integrated into your overall business strategy – it needs to be grounded in the marketplace reality and your business' unique value or selling proposition (Or USP as it has been called since the 1940's.) A well designed profit-generating website starts with a plan based on researched data and your company goals.

Gather the following information before you launch your internet strategy:

A. **Know your customers:** Your website layout, design and contents are going to be solely influenced by your customers' expectations and needs. You first need to start with researching and gathering information to help you execute your strategy and optimise results. Here is some basic information that is needed before you launch your internet strategy:

    1. How old are they?
    2. What cultures do they come from?
    3. Where do they live?
    4. What is the household income, size of family?
    5. What professions do they engage in?
    6. What is their lifestyle like?
    7. What are their beliefs?
    8. What are their radio/TV watching habits?

What are their buying habits?

    1. What are their hot buttons issues that your products or services address? (Zero in on their biggest problems.)
    2. How do they use your products/services?
    3. How often do they use your products/services?
    4. How much money do they spend?
    5. What are their expectations from the products/services that you offer?

What are my prospects' internet usages behaviours like?

    1. What percent of your prospects look for your type of product/service on the internet *vs.* Yellow Pages?
    2. What keywords or key phrases do they use to search products or services similar to that which you offer?
    3. What percent of your prospects purchase your product/service over the internet?
    4. What makes them decide to buy on the web vs. in a store?

STEP II: Identify Keywords

You must find the keywords that your customers use to find your products/services through search engines. Your customers will typically find your products or services by searching for a particular keyword or key-phrase on search engines like Google, Yahoo & MSN. Internet users are getting more sophisticated every day, and have learned to use keywords that give them the best results for what they seek.

Small businesses with a local presence and prospects can be found by using keywords or key-phrases and adding their locality. For example, keyword "Realtor" is very generic and would probably bring websites of national players, or organisations related to the Real Estate business. However, a consumer is typically looking for a real estate agent (Realtor) in a specific area like Irvine, CA, and they know that they do not need a "Realtor" but a "Realtor in Irvine, CA"; hence they are more likely to use "Realtor in Irvine" key-phrase for their search rather than "Realtor" as a keyword. These help a local Irvine, California Realtor plan and compete for the "Realtor in Irvine" key-phrase. Here are some ideas to build a massive list of keywords for your website:

    A. Visit competitors' websites and check their titles and meta-tags. (Meta-tags help search engines index a website for specific keyword podcasts sending contents [text/video/audio to specific equipment (cell phones, Ipods, etc. through the internet)]

    B. Check your customers' testimonials to see what keywords they use. This will also help you build a customer-centric keyword list.

    C. Check all synonyms – use a good Thesaurus

    D. Use both singular and plural keywords.

    E. Use hyphenation and variation – I.E. Off-shore, offshore.

    F. Use domain names of other businesses – I.E. CNN.

    G. Use tools available for keyword identification.

Some tools are:

    ✯ Fee Based (for most comprehensive list of keywords and key phrases used for your products/services:

1. Word Tracker (www.wordtracker.com)
2 Trellian (www.keyworddiscovery.com)
☆ Free Services (adequate for most small businesses needs)
1 Yahoo Search Marketing (www.inventory.overture.com)
2 7 Search.com (www.7search.com/KST)
3 Use abbreviations and misspellings of popular keywords
4 Use acronyms. You can find acronyms at acronym generator, www.acronymfinder.com.
5 Combine keyword phrases to one – Ex. Vitamins and herbs, vitamins and herbs and vitaminsandherbs
6 Use "+" with keywords – Ex. vitamins+herbs
7 Visit crossword compiler, plug keywords and identify additional words. Check www.crossword-compile.com and other similar websites.
8 Use permutation/combination of keywords – Ex. Affordable website design and design affordable website. Check sites like www.keywordtumbler.com.

Building a keywords list is not a one-time process; it changes with. consumer usage behaviour. Focus on the keywords being used currently to start your website and make adjustments as the usage behavior changes.

WEBSITE DESIGN Don'ts:

1 Designing too much animation and too many flashing objects into your website – Too much flash distracts a visitor from the key message of the site.
2 Putting all products/services you offer in one page – Consumers are typically looking for a unique product or service over the web. Over 80% of the searches are done through keywords. Putting all of your products/services on a page would take the focus away from the particular item that a visitor is looking for. Create a unique landing page for each product or service to maximise sales from your site.
3 Asking visitor to download program in order to see your site – People are distrustful of downloading anything from sites they do not know. If you ask them to download something in order to view your site, a vast majority will move on to other sites.

4. Making them scroll sideways to see the entire page – Make sure the whole content of the web page fits on the screen.
5. Adding frames – Website built in frames are currently not searchable through search engines.
6. Allowing "Under Construction" pages – This is the most complained about feature of any website. If a web page is incomplete, do not show it.
7. Optimising web pages for keywords – The biggest mistake you can make is to optimise a page for keywords for a higher search engine ranking. Always optimise the page for your visitor first, then figure out how to make it search engine friendly.
8. Putting in too many graphics – This will slow your site considerably and typically does not help convert a visitor to a buyer.
9. Allowing your website design to be managed by a programmer – Would you let a printer write copy or design creative work for your brochure? If not, why would you let a programmer design a website for you? Let a marketing professional design the site and write web page contents.

STEP III: Getting Visitors to Your Website

If you thought that creating your website is complex, getting visitors to your website is exponentially more difficult than creating the site. However, as you will see below, your success in driving traffic to the site starts with the website design. Over 80% of all visits to websites occur through search engines when searchers type a keyword or key phrase to Identify websites. The rest of the visits are from people who know your site or have seen traditional advertisement that mentions your site.

Getting Visitors Through Website Advertising:

Below are some tactics that would bring visitors to your website:

Visitors obtained through search engine:

There are three ways you can get these visits –

1. Organic search visits – by making sure that your website shows up in the generic search for keywords that your

prospects use when looking for your products or services. [Organic is another way of saying algorithm= which is a list of very clear instructions for accomplishing some task.
2   Visits through internet advertisement.
3   Popularising your site through traditional marketing

You typically need to use both processes to optimise visits to your website.

Organic search visits –

You accomplish this by making sure that your prospects find you on the search engine results. Search engines design robots that scour the internet and index websites for specific keyword or keyphrase relevance. Once the web page is indexed for specific keywords, search engines rank the page in comparison to other web pages and give it a specific rank. The page is shown in sequence to its rank for the keyword. For example, if a web page is ranked 67, the web page will show up 7th on the 7th page for the keyword.

All engines use its specific algorithm to index and rank a web page. Research suggests that almost 100% of consumers never go beyond the third page of the generic searches for a keyword. A vast majority would go to the second page only if they do not find a relevant site on the first page. If the search engines are doing their job right, then a consumer should always find relevant sites on the first page – which makes it absolutely critical to show up in the first page for relevant keywords. Competition for higher ranking is usually fierce; with the number of web pages for a keyword can be just a few dozen to hundreds of millions. You will obviously find it much easier to get your site on thefirst page for keywords with few web pages vs. ones with millions of web pages. As a result, it makes sense to identify the keywords used by your customers and try to get your site at least on the first page of the search engine for as many relevant keywords as possible.

FACTORS THAT AFFECT SEARCH ENGINE WEBPAGE RANKING

Domain Name – Your website address can be a tell tale sign of what your site is about – both to consumers and search engines.

Unless you have millions of dollars to educate customers regarding what you are about (like amazon.com did), you may want to make your website address explain what you do. For example, suppose you want to start an ecommerce website to sell cell phones. You are better off naming the site cellphones.com. If you check, you will find that the address is taken. But a name like yournamecelphoneestore.com will be most likely available. The name clearly tells a consumer and search engine robots what to Expect on your site.

Design components – Once someone (a customer or a search engine crawler) visits your website, your site should be designed such that it makes it clear that this is a cell phone ecommerce site. You can simply design the site with pictures of phones for sale with description (since search engines typically do not read pictures, you will need to describe the picture with an "alt attribute" for the search engine robots), and steps for purchasing cell phones on your site. [Most search engines interpret the meaning of objects by analysing their alt attribute.] Designing the site to clearly convey its intent is absolutely critical for higher search engine ranking and would result in better sales from the website.

Search Engine Optimisation (SEO)

SEO is the process of increasing the number of visitors to a website by ranking high in the search results of a search engine. The higher a website ranks in the results of a search, the greater the chance that that site will be visited by a user. Your website needs to be optimised to get found when your prospects are searching for your products/services by using a keyword. Below are some ideas for optimising your site for search engines: (optimise means to make as good or useful as possible.)

1. Get your website ready for optimisation:
    a. Create a sitemap for your website
    b. Add a Google sitemap on your website
    c. Make sure that your coding is not blocking search engine robots from crawling the site.

d. Describe all pictures on the site in the source code of the Page. (alt-attribute)
2. Identify the keywords that your prospects use to find your products or services.

   Identify the competitiveness of each keyword by –

   A. Checking the number of Webpages containing keyword

   B. Use tools provided by sites like www.wordtracker.com to identify competitiveness.

Identify keywords with least competition and target those for optimisation first.

3. Create separate landing pages for each keyword and add them to your website. Make sure that there is a link from your keyword-centric page to your homepage, and all pages are listed in the site map of your website.

   ☆ A page title that includes the keyword/key-phrase

   ☆ A page description (below the title) that briefly describes the page and includes keywords in the text

   ☆ Copy that explains your service (in bullet form to make it easy to scan). The copy should contain keyword/key-phrase whenever appropriate.

   ☆ Call to action (what you want a visitor to do)

   ☆ A well written web page will get a higher page ranking from search engines and will also maximise sales to the website visitors.

4. Make sure the keyword is in the first paragraph of the copy and around 2% of the text in the first paragraph should be keywords. Google especially expects around 2% of the copy content to be a keyword for indexing the page for it.

5. Make sure that the source code of all webpages has an appropriate title, description, keyword meta-tags, and alt-tag; and is consistent with the webpage content.

6. Use keyword hyperlink – Word linked to another page that has additional content using the keyword. Search

engines usually follow the links and may credit the site if the page hyperlinked to a keyword is highly relevant for it.
7. Submit all keyword centric webpage URLs to search engines; in addition to the homepage URL.
8. Include your website in your industry-specific directories and trade sites. This increases relevancy of your site for the specific industry in search engine eyes.
9. Add RSS feed in each webpage for the appropriate keyword and bring in relevant information related to the keyword from other sites (RSS is a technical term used to describe feed formats used to publish digital content that is being updated on a frequent basis—such as blogs, news feeds and podcasts.)
10. Create a Blog for each keyword and write Blogs regularly. If you are pressed for time, get it written regularly from writers who will ghostwrites for you. Make sure that your webpage address is mentioned in the Blogs. See the Blog section in this book for details of how to create and market your Blog.
11. Regularly write and post press releases about relevant issues for your business and post it in the press release boards. Make sure your website address is included in the copy of the press release.
12. Join relevant forums and mention your webpage address when appropriate.
13. Add content to the webpage regularly.
14. Generate incoming links to your webpage from other websites. Search engines take it as a vote of confidence when other sites point to your site; especially from well-ranked sites.
15. List your web page in directories and get incoming links to your web page from other related websites.
16. Monitor page ranking of each keyword regularly and track progress.
17. Check sites that show up on page one of search engine and analyse what they are doing different.

Social Networking

> **Tipoff**
>
> Doing the steps above may not bring you in the first page of search engines for all keywords; but you will be successful for enough keywords to make your website extremely profitable.
>
> Now most of the users who have setup their websites already will earn more than Rs.27398 per day… If not you are welcome to the next section of this Book.

Chapter 5

Affiliate Marketing

The most powerful money making system is Affiliate Marketing. This is a very simple concept and after reading some pages of this book you will be able to become an Affiliate Marketer.

Definition – Affiliate means 'to join' and to join somebody in Market for profit is called Affiliate Marketing.

We shall simply learn the concept of Affiliate Marketing by this example:

Suppose there are two persons with three different websites on the Internet:

- ✯ Person A has Good Reputation for His Products but due to Poor SEO or some other reasons there are less visitors to his website and therefore his Profit is going down.
- ✯ Person B does not have any Product to Market on his website, but fortunately his website is famous and a good number of visitors visit and access his website regularly. Say he is running some famous blog, but he is not making Profits too.

Now What Can Be Done?

If Person A and Person B make a Partnership that Person B will promote Person A's link on his website, and for every Purchase made by customer resulting from the click on Person B's website, Person A will give 10% of his profit to Person A. In this way both the sides get benefited.

So, this is the concept of Affiliate Marketing.

PERSON A   PERSON B

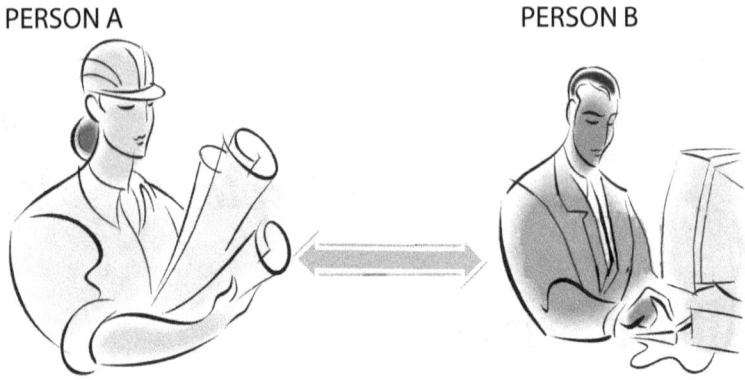

(10,000 Visitors/day)   (1000 Visitors/day)
(Owns Non-Profit Site)   (Owns Profit Site)

After Partnership for Affiliate Marketing

(URL of Person B will be   (Person B will now receive
shown by him)   more visitors)

Visitors from Person A link's will buy products from Person B website

In exchange for every sale made Person B pays 10% commission to Person A.

In the above case both the Partners were initially not getting Profits but after Affiliate Marketing Partnership both of them are enjoying profits.

Now how will you start Affiliate Marketing?

Now you own your blog and websites, no matter whether you are getting huge traffic or not, you can tie up with advertisers, companies and Organisations for Affiliate Marketing.

Visit a website of any famous Brand which support online marketing, click on the tab of "Become an affiliate" follow the guidelines, and fill the fields on the webpage and sign up for becoming an affiliate. They will send you your unique link for affiliation, Place the Link on your website. Next time whenever a visitor clicks on the vary link and buy products from them you will receive a payout on your PayPal account.

Now you already earn 10 blogs, and maybe you have made 50 posts in those blogs or websites. Now sign up for 50 Affiliation Approvals by different brands, get your unique links, place them on your website and you will start earning in matter of seconds.

Calculate your Profit:

Suppose a Product costs Rs.500 and you have signed up for getting 5% commissions, you will get Rs.25 on each sale. So in total you have 10 blogs and 50 links, if only one visitor click on each of the link then you can get 25 X 50 = Rs.1250 per day. And this is the sum of money for only one click per link, and if you get at least 10 clicks you will get Rs.12500 per day!

> **Tipoff**
>
> Please choose your Brand carefully. Please aware of spam here. Don't Select the brand which promises more than 15% commissions.
>
> Make more blogs to earn more....!

Chapter 6

Social Networking: Money Printing Machine

Some Tips Before the Main Content

Organisations have a lot to consider once they decide they want to jump into social networks and social media. There are many opportunities to slide off the rails, or worse, to let the effort fall into disarray. Here are some thoughts based on a question I received recently in email about guidelines, a toolbox, and how to grow a community.

Start with the IntentFirst, know what the intent of your social media and networks will be. Are you hoping to improve awareness and open communication about your organisation? Are you looking to reach new markets and open channels for sales or membership or market adoption? Are you hoping to use these tools as collaboration platforms? Are you making informational products? Are you just virtualising your water cooler?

Knowing your intent drives which path you take.

Treat your community like adults, companies and organisations are most worried about how blogs and podcasts and wikis will be used. The truth is, most employee code of conduct policies cover this related to email use. It's not much different. Don't add another thousand rules as to what should go on within the social networks, except insofar as what differences come with the medium. For example, don't bury people in what not to say. If you're a publicly traded company, let them add a disclaimer to the blog (strictly my opinions), remind them about the email policy, and let it go.

A Sample Blogging Policy

If I were launching a social media program at a company, I'd hold a quick meeting in person. I'd mention the following:

- ✭ We're opening up blogging to the organisation. Everyone here is now invited to use our new blogging platform. Why do this? Because we think you're creative, intelligent people, and we want to give you a chance to share your ideas with a larger audience, inside and outside the organisation.

- ✭ As this is public, just remember that we can't talk about company secrets, upcoming projects that aren't yet public, or anything that could impact our company's stock value.

- ✭ Within reason, you can say what you think about our publicly released products and services. If you're critical of something, recommend solutions. Offer examples of improvements. We'd prefer it to be constructive. Use your judgment.

- ✭ When posting pictures or movies or music, understand that some materials may be copyrighted. For instance, just because you can see a picture on a Google Image Search or find it in Flickr, that doesn't mean you have rights to post it on your blog. We'll talk more about Creative Commons and some other resources later.

- ✭ It's fine to post "off-topic." We don't expect every single post to be about the organisation. We hope you'll talk about us from time to time, as our goal is showing our customers, vendors, and other stakeholders, as well as the community at large, that you are what makes our company amazing.

- ✭ Mentioning our competitors is fine. The world doesn't revolve around us (okay, we pretend it does!), and we

know that some people do some aspects of what we do better. Don't rub our noses in it, but we get it.
- ★ Deleting blog posts is considered bad etiquette on the web. We won't do it here, unless something violates our privacy policies, and/or our ethics policies. Posting hotties probably won't fly, but the occasional cute picture of your cat in a cowboy hat is okay. You're a real human, not a robot.
- ★ Did we mention it'd be cool if you talked about us once in a while?

Great!
- ★ It's considered good etiquette to link to other great posts you read, and to comment on other blogs written by people you admire or want to engage in conversation.
- ★ As for how often or how much is too much, and things like that, around here, we measure you on your results at your primary function. If your work starts suffering on your way to the A list of bloggers, we'll have to adjust your expectations a little bit. Otherwise, use your judgment.

Elements of Your Social Media Platform

People are selling all kinds of technology for blogging. Even when there are plenty of free and open source platforms out there. Even simple hosted opportunities abound. Beyond that, there are some great new collaborative products, and TONS of content management software companies out there making all flavour of solution. So, instead of recommending any specific platform, I'll point out some things to consider:
- ★ Operating environments vary: Several content systems work on Linux platforms, using solely open source, and others are built for a Windows environment. If you're building the system in-house, consider what your IT team will be comfortable supporting. Or, bypass both camps entirely and build on a hosted environment out on the web, but this is a consideration.

Social Networking

- Related to the last point, the more arcane or unknown the system, the less likely it will be for you to find support, should the vendor and you fall out of love. Be wary of that.
- The content system should feature RSS feed support. This means that all the content can be exported via a specific protocol that allows people to view it in a reader or other application of their choice, and not just at the website as a destination. (For me, systems that don't support RSS are a show-stopper. You might have a different opinion).
- The ability to post in a simple visual manner (that would feel like using a tool like Microsoft Word) as well as the ability to post in HTML format is useful. I like writing in HTML, but others might prefer the comfort of the WYSIWYG tools.
- Media support is fairly standard these days, but should be considered. In a world where YouTube isn't just skateboarding dogs any more, the ability to embed Flash video, as well as the ability to post MP3 and MOV files (amongst other types) would be important.
- Video has lots of added challenges. I strongly recommend a 3rd party hosting platform, and then embedding a player instead of integrating to your platform. Yes, there are great platforms working inside the firewall, and there are some easy add-on video solutions, but if you're going to go heavy into video and aren't a production or media company, that's a part probably best outsourced.
- Is mobile a priority? There are applications like Utterz and Tumblr and more who allow for mobile posting. Integrating input from more than one source would thereby also be important and of interest. Pay attention to how easy it is to import feeds and post into your media platform. This is one limitation that can be somewhat vexing later on.
- Backing up, exporting, importing, and some administrative functions are important to consider, if you're going to put any serious data and effort into the platform. For example, I do full backups of the data on [chrisbrogan.com] every

week, regardless of the fact that it's posted on a hosting system.
- ☆ Customisation is important. If you can't make the platform look and feel like the rest of your presence, what's the point? Most systems accommodate for this rather well, permitting CSS (Cascading Style Sheet) support and other features, but make sure.
- ☆ Beyond this, there are lots of "your mileage may vary" opinions, but this should be a good start.

Keeping a Community Alive and Growing It

I saved the hardest part for last. In that old Kevin Costner movie, Field of Dreams, the tagline/hook of the movie was a ghostly voice in the cornfields saying, "If you build it, they will come." Nothing is farther from the truth. People's attention spans are frayed to their very edges. Work stresses are equally ramped up. The "shiny new thing" quotient on the web is at its highest right now. So the odds of making a full, fat, rich robust community that swells into the hundreds of thousands overnight is fairly slim. For every "overnight" success like Club Penguin for kids or Facebook for everyone else, there are tons of digital ghost towns out there. I'm not about to say that I know what the secret ingredient is, because if I did, I'd make my own network, and get Microsoft and Google to bid me up to the billions and retire to New found land. Here, instead, are some thoughts.

- ☆ Communities that have "something to do" better. Want an example?
- ☆ *Amazon*. You can go there and review books, write comments, build wikis, and do a million other things around products you love. Another? *Flickr*. Go there and look at other people's photos, join groups, tag and comment and make notes. *Facebook*. You could get lost in all the time wasting applications, or get deeply involved in all the groups there. Make sure there's something to do.
- ☆ Go outside the borders often. New communities grow by gently encouraging new immigrants. For example, if you're

active on Twitter, you can occasionally point to posts on your new community. Not always. That gets boring quick. You can comment on other blogs that are similar to your group's intent, and where you populate your URL (in most blogs, you enter your name, email, and URL). Folks click on the URL of comments that seem interesting. (Don't spam!)

- Encourage more than you stifle. You want to see a community turn on their keepers? When sites go astray of their community-minded goals, bad things happen. Look at what happened when social news site Digg changed their algorithm a bit. It wasn't pretty. So be wary of how you interact with the community.

- Make it worth for the community. If you're going to build a place for people to collaborate and share ideas and build content, be on the lookout for ways to give something to your community for their efforts.

- Administrators are not community managers. Community managers exist out there who know all the great ways to engage people. Connie Bensen, Jake McKee, Jeremiah Owyang, and a host of other great people are community types to their very bones. They know how to energise a community. Seek out a community manager to run the environment, and make it their primary role. This is worth TONS in the long run.

Other People's Networks

Here is one consideration for when to build your own social network and when to use existing social networks: A. whether you have an abundance of community around your organisation already *vs.* B. if you are seeking to grow a community. If it's A, then build a social network. If you're looking to grow from nothing, consider starting in B (other people's social networks).

I use both for my own interests. I think it's important to be part of the community at large, and so I participate on Twitter, to a lesser extent on Facebook, and then in a variety of other places. My personal method is to focus on the people, not the platform, meaning that I'm not on Facebook because it's Facebook. I'm there because some of my friends and business colleagues are there. That's a popular Eric Rice warning to social networks, too. He goes where his crowd is, not just to the new and shiny thing. For you, it's mostly a question of whether you have the community in place and are looking for a targeted place within your platform to offer them tools and resources to connect and cross-communicate. One of the current best-of-breed examples of this is FastCompany.com, who turned their online property into a social network around their magazine's points of business, instead of a rehash of their magazine. Points go to USAToday.com for their effort, too. Is there a hybrid model? I think so. You can perhaps build a network and understand that it might be slow to grow, and then grow your community by participating in "outpost" areas like Facebook or Twitter or the other two billion networks that are out there.

People are the Core

At the core of this are people. Everything that has come before this doesn't work a lick until you understand the people you intend to reach, the people you hope will contribute, and the people who will share their time with you on all angles. If, for instance, you start a blogging platform at work, and then complain that people are using it, they won't use it. If you build a social network dedicated to talking about how great your company or products are, that will get old really fast.

Do you know humankind's greatest need? The need to feel wanted. If you consider the incentives behind most people's actions in a given day (especially mean people), what's at the core of it is to feel that they're doing something important, interesting, and worthwhile. That has to be at the centre of your motivations and perspective if you're launching a project like this. Make it worth it for the people, and they will participate.

Now, Just Start

Analysis paralysis is a terrible thing. Just try something. Even if you launch a really small part of your project's intentions, now is the right time to try. What's holding you back?

Tip off

Now you are going to learn two new things – Facebook and LinkedIn. We will only tell you how to earn money using these networks.

It is very important to read it thrice before starting the next chapters.

Chapter 7

Basic Facebook

Introduction to Facebook

What is Facebook?

Founded in February 2004, Facebook is a social network that helps people communicate more efficiently with their friends, family, co-workers and acquaintants. The company develops technologies that facilitate the sharing of information through the digital mapping of people's real-world social connections. Anyone can sign up for Facebook, and in fact, 400 million people are already on Facebook. The average user spends more than 55 minutes per day on Facebook. So, what are these users doing for 55 minutes per day? More importantly, how can conservative activists use this network to find like-minded activists and organise around a cause digitally? We're going to tell you, so read on!

Who started Facebook?

Mark Zuckerberg founded Facebook with his college roommates and fellow computer science students Eduardo Saverin, Dustin Moskovitz and Chris Hughes while he was a student at Harvard University.

The website's membership was initially limited to Harvard students, but it later expanded further to include any university student. In late 2005, it was open to high school students, and finally, in 2006, Facebook became available to anyone aged 13 and over with a valid e-mail address. Facebook was once only available through a computer, however, in 2006 applications became available that make Facebook available through mobile phones, PDAs, iPods and other mp3 devices. There are more than 65 million active users currently accessing Facebook through their mobile devices.

Zuckerberg

Interesting Facts about Facebook

- ☆ More than 400 million active users
- ☆ 50% of our active users log on to Facebook in any given day
- ☆ More than 35 million users update their status each day
- ☆ More than 60 million status updates posted each day
- ☆ More than 3 billion photos uploaded to the site each month
- ☆ More than 5 billion pieces of content (links, news stories, blog posts, notes, photo albums, etc.)
- ☆ shared each week
- ☆ More than 3.5 million events created each month
- ☆ More than 3 million active Pages on Facebook

Basic Facebook

- More than 1.5 million local businesses have active Pages on Facebook
- More than 20 million people become fans of Pages each day
- Pages have created more than 5.3 billion fans
- An average user has 130 friends on the site
- An average user sends 8 friend requests per month
- An average user spends more than 55 minutes per day on Facebook
- An average user clicks the Like button on 9 pieces of content each month
- An average user writes 25 comments on Facebook content each month
- An average user becomes a fan of 4 Pages each month
- An average user is invited to 3 events per month
- An average user is a member of 13 groups

Getting on Facebook
Setting up a Facebook account

So you decided to take the plunge and create a Facebook account! You are not alone. There are over 400 million people on this social networking website! In fact, if Facebook were a country, it would be the third most populated country in the world, only behind India and China (impressive or scary, depending on how you look at it).Steps to creating an account:

1. Write the URL Facebook.com

2. Provide your first and last names, an e-mail address, birthday and gender. Finally, create a password, something you will remember, but tough enough so that it won't be easily determined. We suggest using at least 11 digits, with at least 3 numbers, substituting symbols for letters (like "!" for "I"). If you are a married woman, it might be easier for old friends to find you if you use your maiden name for Facebook.
3. Facebook will ask you to complete your profile by asking for your high school, college and employer. You may skip this step, but we encourage you to provide information for one or all of the categories. This will help Facebook users find and identify you.
4. Finally, they will ask you to provide a photo. You can upload a photo already on your computer or by using a webcam, or skip this step until you find a picture you  like. When selecting an image, remember that Facebook gives you 200px in width and up to 600px in height. If larger, Facebook will crop your image down to fit 200px, keeping the same height ratio. If you do not provide an image, you will get Facebook's lovely default: *The Coolwhip Man*
5. If prompted to add friends from your e-mail contacts, skip over this process for now. We will come back to this later. Facebook will send you a confirmation e-mail to the account you provided. Once your account is confirmed, you are ready to find your old friends and start making new ones.

Facebook Profile

Re-visit Facebook.com and log in using your e-mail address and the password you created. Once logged in, you will see

Basic Facebook

that Facebook has prepared you to begin finding friends. But, before you do this, we encourage you to begin building your Facebook Profile (the information others will see about you). Click on the My Profile link in the upper left hand corner to get started.

Vanity URLs

One of the most overlooked, but extremely valuable resources is Facebook's Vanity URL feature. Most Facebook Profiles are indexed online as http://www.facebook.com/profile.php?id=1591575650 but this makes it very hard to find and share your profile with others. Facebook makes it easy to shorten this to a more manageable and attractive URL. To secure your vanity URL, visit http://www.facebook.com/username/. This can also be utilised for Pages and Groups, which we will discuss later in this book.

Updating your Profile's Information

1. Once you have successfully navigated to your profile, click the Information tab next to your image.
2. You will see a series of Edit buttons at the top right corner. Start with your basic information first, making sure you pay close attention to what you want to provide and who you want to be. For instance, politicos may choose to be very specific with political belifes. Those wanting privacy may choose to give very little personal information.
3. Continue down the page, clicking the Edit buttons at the top-right of the information boxes. Your personal profile

has four different sections: basic information, personal information, contact information, and education and work.

Your profile will be where others come to learn about you, so it is important to be honest. For example, if you enjoy reading, be sure to elaborate on the type of books; we guarantee you will quickly meet a new friend who shares your passion for *Harry Potter*.

Finding Friends

Now that you have fleshed out your Facebook identity, it is time to start adding friends.

Using the navigation at the top-right of your screen, click the Home button. If you skipped over the "finding friends" portion, you will likely see the option to search through your e-mail contacts. This section will look similar to the image below:

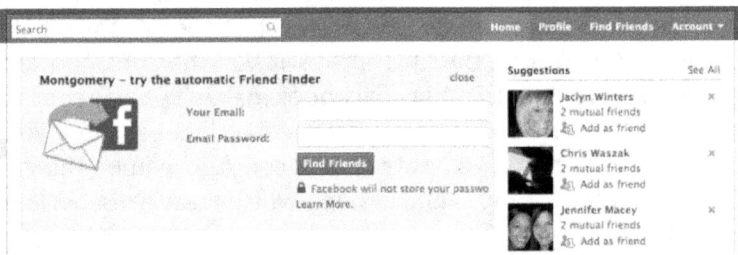

We recommend allowing Facebook to search through your e-mail contacts to find friends who have setup accounts. Facebook will quickly locate them and allow you to connect, or "become friends." Facebook does not save your e-mail password anywhere, using it only once and deleting it.

You can find additional friends by dropping down the Account link in the top right of your page. Once expanded, you will see the option to Edit Friends. Facebook's Edit Friends page will allow you several options to find and connect with people you may know online: use your e-mail address book, phonebook, or find friends through other instant messaging applications.

Basic Facebook

Navigation on Facebook
The Layout

Once you have built your profile and have gathered a few friends, it is time to get acquainted with all that Facebook has to offer. Knowing where to find everything on your Facebook account is very important. Not only will it save your time, but most people do not completely understand all that Facebook offers. We will start at the very top left corner, with the Facebook logo.

Facebook Icon

Clicking the Facebook icon will take you back to your home page (we will discuss your Home when we get to the "Home" link in the navigation). To the right of the Facebook icon is three silhouetted icons. The first is a link to your Friend Requests.

Friend Suggestions

Here you will quickly see a list of friends who want to connect with you. In addition, Facebook has added some Friend Suggestions to the list, people who Facebook thinks you will get along with or with whom you share mutual interests.

Search

This is a very important tool for beginners and newcomers to Facebook. You can quickly search for brands, organisations, and friends via this text box. Simply type in the name of a local tea party, 9/12, or other group/friend to find and connect with them on Facebook. Next to the search box you will see your Home button.

Home

This is one of the most useful areas of Facebook. Your Home page will display a snapshot of important information for you to

Social Networking

take advantage of (please note that your homepage is not your profile page, which we will discuss momentarily).

To the left, you will see a list of events, messages, photos, and other things that may require your attention.

Directly below that you can find those friends that are online. This is an interesting feature that allows you quickly chat with friends via Facebook's chat feature, located at the bottom right of your screen. The pop-up box functions like an instant message feature, allowing you to quickly communicate with others who are online.

Moving to the far right, Facebook displays all requests for your account. From events that friends would like you to attend to groups that would like for you to join, you can look through invitations here. In addition, Facebook uses the space below these requests to display pages that Facebook thinks you would find interesting (more on Facebook pages later).

Basic Facebook

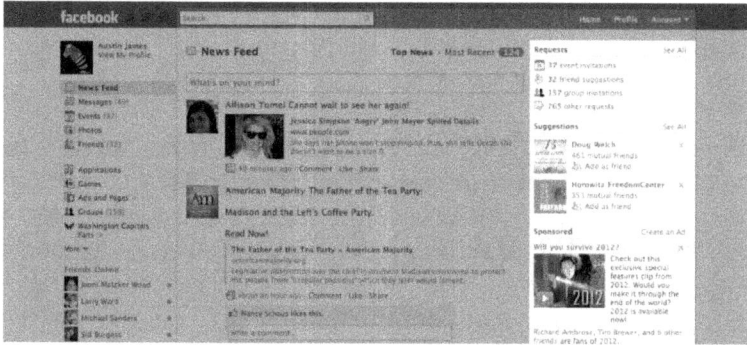

Also on the far right, you will find sponsored ads, an extended list of events, and an out-dated feature called "Poking" that serves little purpose and should be ignored. In the middle of the Home page is where you will find your News Feed, one of the most valuable functions of Facebook.

News Feed

Your News Feed is an updated list of what your friends are doing and posting. This section is broken up into two portions: Top News and Most Recent.

Top News

This is a live update to what your most popular friends are doing. Those friends that you interact with most will show up in this list. When they post an update, share a photo, link, or video,

Social Networking

it will be displayed here. Facebook automatically places the friends you interact with most into this display

Most Recent

Here you will find all of your friends' updates, regardless of how many times you have interacted with them. When clicking on the most recent button, you will be taken to an updated stream of statuses and other activity by all of your friends on Facebook. Facebook has broken your news feed into two manageable portions so you can focus on your most valuable contacts or see all of your Facebook friends.

The second text link is entitled "Profile". Clicking this will take you to your personal profile. Here you can view and edit the information discussed earlier in the guide.

The final link in your navigation is the Account button, which houses a drop down feature that leads to seven more links. These links are discussed on the next page.

Edit Friends

This page allows you to manage your friends. Here you can delete friends, find more, and manage your friends in lists (a feature we will talk more about later).

Account Settings

Here you can edit a multitude of different functions. You can manage what notifications Facebook sends you, connect

Basic Facebook

Facebook to a mobile device, buy Facebook Ads, and make

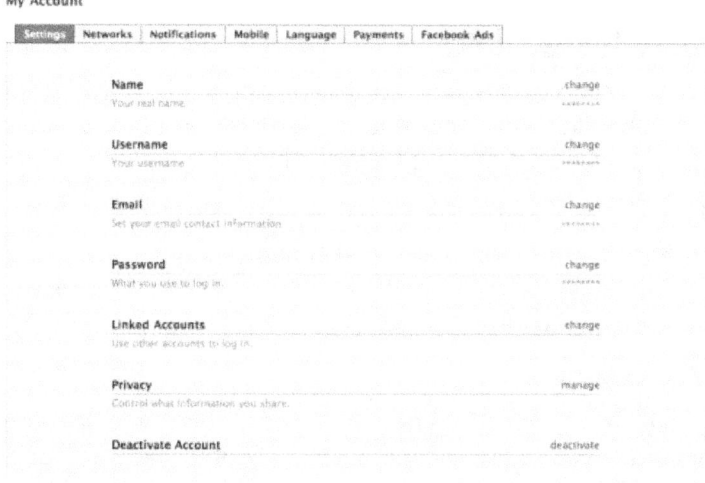

many other changes.

Privacy Settings

Perhaps one of the most overlooked settings in Facebook is your ability to protect your privacy. Privacy is one of the key differentiators of Facebook from other social networking services. Facebook gives you the option to control what others see, right down to individual photo albums, or various pieces of personal information such as your address, phone number, and screen name on instant messaging services. There are several

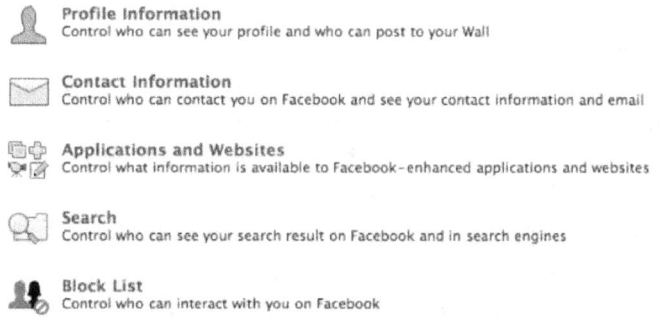

very good resources to help you keep your information private, so we will not go intoall of the setting here.

Application Settings

Here you can manage how third-party applications will interact with your Facebook information. Settings on photos, events, groups and videos can also be found here.

Credits

The fifth link is credit balance; this allows you to link a Credit Card or Mobile Phone account to your Facebook account in order to purchase Facebook gifts or Credits for online games.

Help Center

If you have any questions not answered in this guide, we highly encourage you to use Facebook's Help Center. There are tons of great articles, questions and answers, and tutorials within this section.

Logout

This should be pretty self-explanatory.

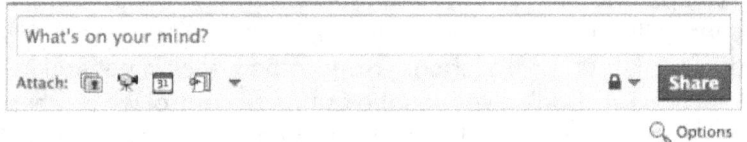

Aspects of your Facebook Account

Wall and Status

To the left of the Information tab we edited earlier, you will find your Wall tab. Your wall is where you and your friends can post content to be shared, such as photos, videos and web links or just a simple message to say "hi".

Using the box at the top of your wall (see above image), you can easily type a message to share with your friends. This is called "updating your status". By updating your status, you are sending

Basic Facebook

a message to all of your friends. This is the easiest way to communicate with your contacts within Facebook. In addition

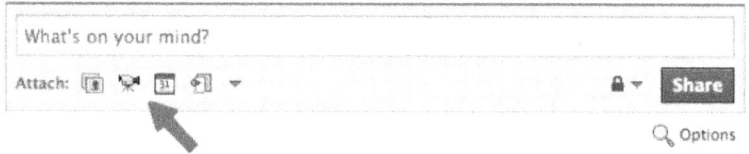

to simple messages, you can use the icons below the text field to attach videos, web links to a blog or news stories, and photos (example below shows how to add video).

The area directly below this text box is referred to as your Wall. Your Wall houses not only your status updates, but also any of

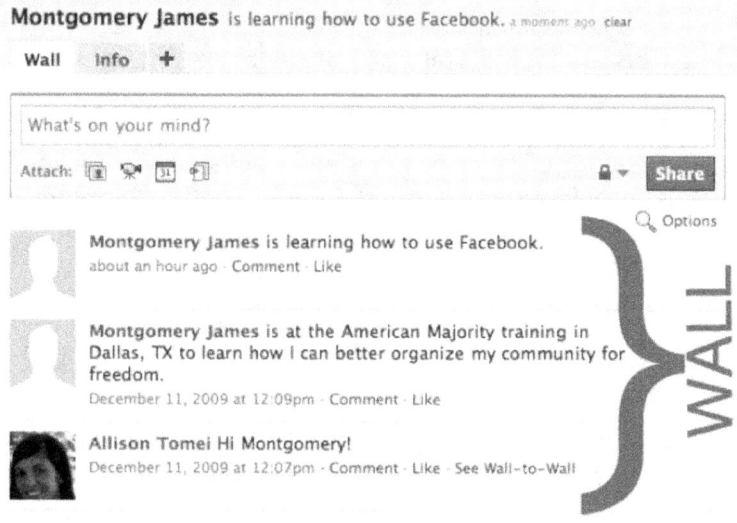

the messages, videos or photos people have shared directly with you.

It is important to note that when you enter something on your own wall, Facebook will insert your name before the message

Social Networking

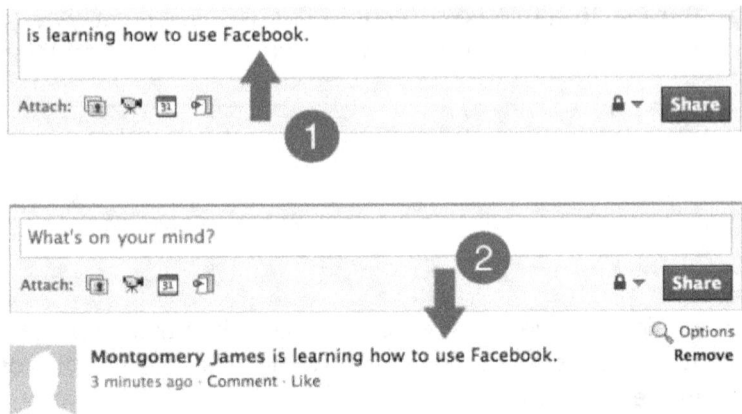

when posted. There is no need to duplicate your name and you can even have a little fun:

1. This is an example of a status update.
2. This is what that status update looks like once posted.

Like/Comment

A new feature of Facebook, added in 2009, allows Facebook friends to quicklyshow support for one another's content by

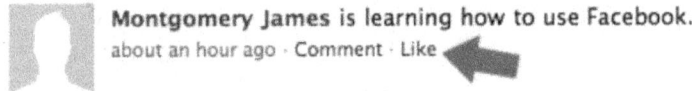

clicking a button letting the others know that the user liked the content. Facebook's "Like" button allows you to increase interaction and reduce the need to write out a message. Simply click the word 'Like' just below a post:

For instance, if you post that you are attending an American Majority training in Kansas, one friend may comment, "I have attended an American Majority training in the past and learned a lot, enjoy!" while another may simply choose to click the "Like" button, indicating their support as well. This feature is especially helpful for activists who post news stories from various websites and blogs. Fellow activists and friends can quickly click the "Like" button, indicating that they like the content and would like to see more. Less clicks means the content might not be right for the community.

Photos

One of Facebook's most used features is its ability to allow users to upload and share photos. The photos can be uploaded from your computer, phone, webcam and other devices. You can create and share individual photos or whole albums, but remember that as with most of Facebook's capabilities, your friends have the ability to comment on your photos once they are uploaded. If you would like to keep photos private, we suggest you do the following:

Go to: Privacy -> Profile -> Basic -> Edit Photo Albums Privacy Settings

Edit privacy settings for each photo you have on your Facebook profile individually. Every single photo can have its privacy settings changed separately. Choose to have everyone see your photo, only networks and friends, friends of friends, only friends or you can customise your privacy settings for each photo. To upload a photo, you have several options. The two most effective options are mobile and profile.

Mobile Uploads

Connect With Friends

 Invite friends to join Facebook.

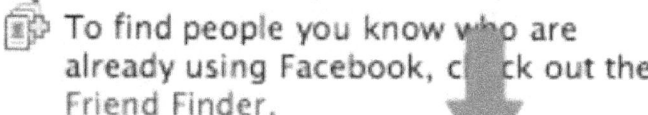 To find people you know who are already using Facebook, check out the Friend Finder.

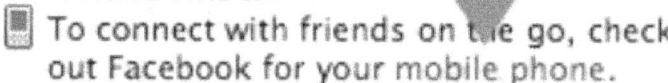 To connect with friends on the go, check out Facebook for your mobile phone.

Social Networking

We will not explore mobile applications here, but do know that if you have a smartphone (Blackberry or iPhone most notably) there are a plethora of options out there. To learn more, visit the link in the bottom-right of your Home page.

You will be taken to a page with information on mobile devices, text messages, and even e-mail updates to your Facebook account. Take the time to explore the material and decide if some of these more advanced options are right for you.

Profile Uploads

Adding photos to your account can be a little daunting at first,

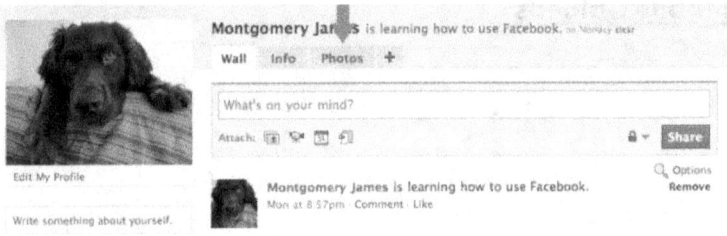

which is why we suggest starting with a manual approach through your Profile page. Below you will see an image of our demo account's Profile. Notice the tab that says "Photos." This is where we want to focus.

Clicking the tab will take you to a page where you can view all of your photos, organise them, and upload new ones. It is important to note that a photo must be in an album. This can be an album you create, or one automatically created by Facebook. For instance, any photo you have used as your Profile photo (the one other friends will see on your Profile page) will be saved in a photo album entitled, "Profile Pictures." Keeping everything in albums helps to streamline and order your photos for others to

enjoy. Likewise, all mobile uploaded photos will be added to a "Mobile" album for you to organise once you are online and the default photo album for all manually added photos is "My Photos".

To help speed up and maximise the efficiency of uploading photos, Facebook recently released a plug-in application that will need to be added to your internet browser (Internet Explorer, Safari, Firefox, etc.) of choice. Once you have clicked on the "Create an Album" you should be prompted to install

this application. Once done, you are ready to start sharing your images with the world!

We also want to reiterate that you can add images to Status Updates (a feature we discussed earlier). Simply click the "photo" icon below your message to add an image from your computer

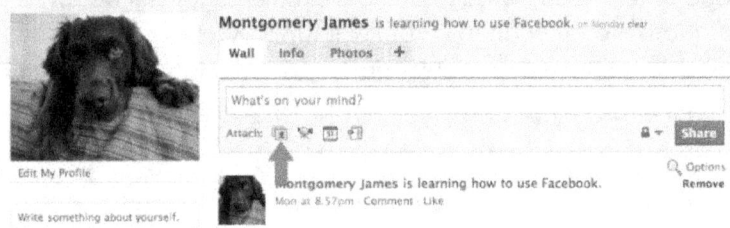

or online.

Messages/Inbox

Facebook's message feature allows you to talk directly and privately with another Facebook user. To access this function, simply click the Message button discussed earlier:

From here, you will be able to quickly access any message sent to you, compose a new message, and view all messages for your account. Messages are a very handy tool. For instance, if you do not want to post a message to your friends' wall because it is personal or you do not want anyone else to see it, you can send them a personal message instead. This ensures that only they see the message. Additionally, you can send a private message to multiple friends. For instance, if you want to send a message to 4 friends in your Tea Party or 9/12 group to set up a carpool to a rally, you can type in each person's name in the subject line and only those 4 people receive the message. You can also attach photos, links or videos in personal messages.

Basic Facebook

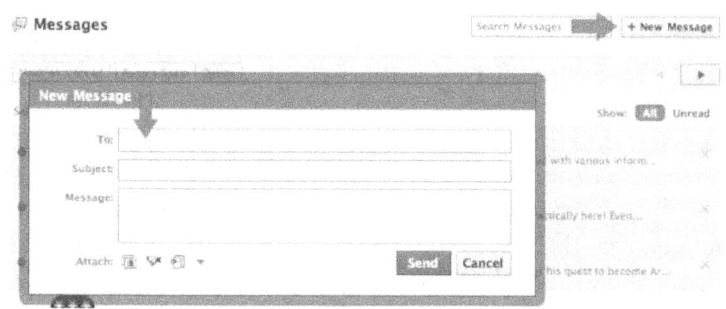

Notes

The notes section does not offer much purpose in today's social network, especially with the rise of personal blogs and other technologies that offer much more customisation and robust latforms. We will gloss over this function for now, but note (pun intended) that you can use notes to post large amounts of text – like a blog – to share with others. The quick and vast nature of facebook is not conducive for using such a time consuming function, but we want you to be aware of it, as some might find it useful for re-posting.

Sharing and Interacting

Facebook is known for more than just keeping old friends in touch. It is also one of the most popular (if not the most popular) places for sharing information. More than 3.5 billion pieces of content (web links, news stories, blog posts, notes, photo albums etc.) are shared each week via Facebook. It provides a platform for not only sharing the information, but also for interacting with the information. Most news or magazine sites online (i.e. CNN, Politico, People Magazine) allow you to send their stories directly to your Facebook wall or to another friend via Facebook message.

Some organisations have this feature on their blog, as well. Facebook has single-handedly increased social sharing, decreasing the information gaps and freeing us from our geographical boundaries.

Social Networking

There are many ways to organise and interact with like-minded people, whether your interest is conservative politics or golden retrievers. Some of the Facebook features that allow users of similar interests to gather in one place are Groups, Events, Fan Pages and Causes. And, in true Facebook interactive fashion, you are able to comment and post content within each of these features. Facebook pages started because Facebook creators noticed that there wasn't a way for users to connect with music artists, brands or other popular groups in our culture. Now, not only can you connect with your favorite artists and businesses, but now you also can show your friends what you care about and recommend by adding the Pages to your personal profile. There are more than 1.6 million active Pages on Facebook and more than 700,000 local businesses have active Pages on Facebook! Continue on to learn more about these unique features.

Chapter 8

Facebook Marketing Tools

Introduction

Facebook is fast becoming a powerhouse of marketing activity due to the sheer numbers of engaged users on the site and the simplicity of connecting with them directly. If you're promoting a business, product, band or some other public figure, you have probably been advised at some point or other to "get a Facebook presence" because "Facebook is huge".

So, How Do you Get Started?

In order to make the best of Facebook for marketing, you'll need to understand the tools available, how they're used, best practices and how to set the tools up. But that's just the start. Once you start piecing together this puzzle you'll be able to manage your marketing efforts across multiple Facebook products with ease and style.

First Things First: Getting Started

Organisations Should Not Create Personal Profiles

Profiles are for individuals only. If you are representing a company, organisation, event or group then register for Facebook as yourself and then create a Facebook Group, Page or Event as appropriate. Later you can (and should) add other individuals from your organisation as co-administrators.

Personal accounts which are deemed to be fake (i.e. not an individual) risk deletion by Facebook. I'm sure this is not something you want to happen to your business, so DO NOT start a personal Facebook account with a business name.

It recently also become has possible to register a Business account purely for administering Pages and advertisements. These accounts are limited, but do have their uses. Read more under "Facebook Pages".

Remember Your Personal Privacy

Note that if you're a figurehead for your company or organisation (as you will be if you are the creator of the Facebook event, group or page) that some users will be keen to find out more about you. This means it is vital for you to ensure your privacy settings on your own personal account are such that you show a professional image and do not expose yourself or your friends to threats or embarrassment.

Keep Work and Play Separate

If you are setting up a Facebook page for work purposes, keep things separate from your friends. Don't ask your Facebook friends to "like" your work's Facebook page; let it grow organically. This is not only best for your business' reputation, but also best for your privacy, professional profile and relationships with your friends.

Administration

We will tell you how to set up Groups, Pages, Networks and Applications as an administrator.

All of these can be accomplished by anyone and you remain logged into Facebook as yourself to do it. Once these things are set up, you can add extra administrators to help manage them. In fact, it's recommended that you do this in order to ensure someone can always manage things effectively. Don't forget to check back regularly and add new admins if you need to.

Group or Page?

Before creating a group or a page, you might want to think about which is best for your needs. Generally, for a public face, Facebook Pages are best. If you're the manager of a big event, organisation, company, movement or product then this is the best choice. If you're co-ordinating a small community group, on the other hand, creating a Facebook Group may be a better idea.

The main differences lie in publicity, statistics and event invitations. Facebook Pages give you regular statistics on follower numbers and demographics. They're also very easy to publicise, using widgets and the viral "like" functionality. However, if you then host an event, you can only publicise it to your fans using an update through the news feed. You can't directly invite people to the event unless you are already friends with them. Facebook Groups, on the other hand, can send event invites to group members.

An example of how both a group and a page may be beneficial is in the instance of a choir, theatre group or other performance-oriented club. For the members of the club, the Facebook Group can keep people informed of club matters, social events and other things important to members and ex-members. The Facebook Page could be used to promote the performances and important news to fans.

Another situation could be for events. The host company and the event could have a fan page, while the management committee, staff and volunteers could be coordinated using groups. Basically, groups are perfect for internal purposes while pages make a great public face.

Facebook Groups

Facebook Groups are now all the "new" groups as of late 2010. These groups are primarily closed to all but the members of the group. They automatically include group chat abilities and an email address, which can be used to communicate with the group as if it were a mailing list.

First, search Facebook to see if the group you're thinking of already exists. If not, head to the groups application via your home page. Right up the top is a "Create a Group" button.

 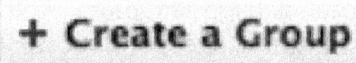

Then you choose the name, members and set the security settings for the group. The most important choice to make is down at the bottom. You need to decide how public this group will be. If you're making the group for a small community of people, then closed is usually the best. People can see it and ask to be approved as a member, but it's kept somewhat private for outsiders. You can change any of these settings later by choosing to edit the group and clicking the customise tab. It's your group, so make decisions as you see fit. If you're not sure, leave the group closed until you know you want it otherwise.

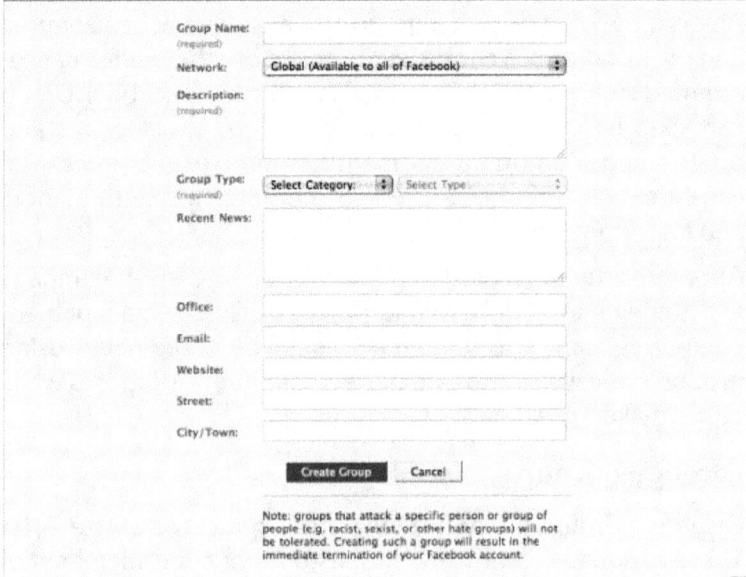

You can later edit the group information. Plug in as much information as you wish.

Facebook Marketing Tools

You're able to choose an email address for the group, so that it can be used in the same way as a group mailing list. You can choose this in the group settings.

Create group email address

Enter an email address for your group.

[   ]@groups.facebook.com

Emails sent to this address will go to all group members.

[Create email address] [Cancel]

Facebook will then let you promote the Group by publishing to your wall or inviting friends. When these people join the group it will show up on their profile wall and news feed of their friends, thus promoting it further.

To make someone an administrator, go to the "Members" tab. Next to each member you'll see an option to "Make Admin". Any

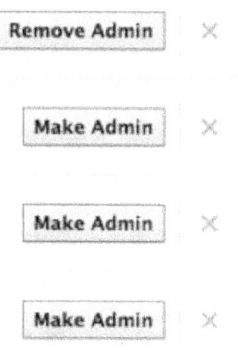

admins can approve new members, edit the group, send messages to everyone and remove other admins (that have been there a shorter amount of time than themselves). I would recommend adding a couple of people you trust as administrators as soon as possible.

Upload a photo for the group at any time by clicking on the group picture in exactly the same way you do it for profile pictures.

Social Networking

Events for Groups

To create an event hosted by a group, go to your group page and click the "Event" link on the status bar.

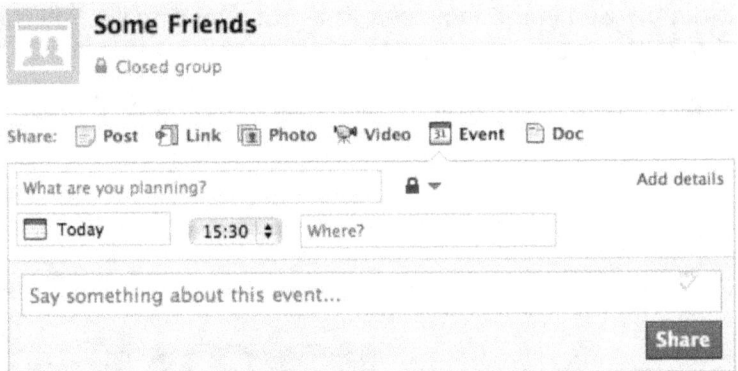

From then on, it's exactly like creating an event by an individual, except that there's a check box which allows you to invite everyone from the host group to the event.

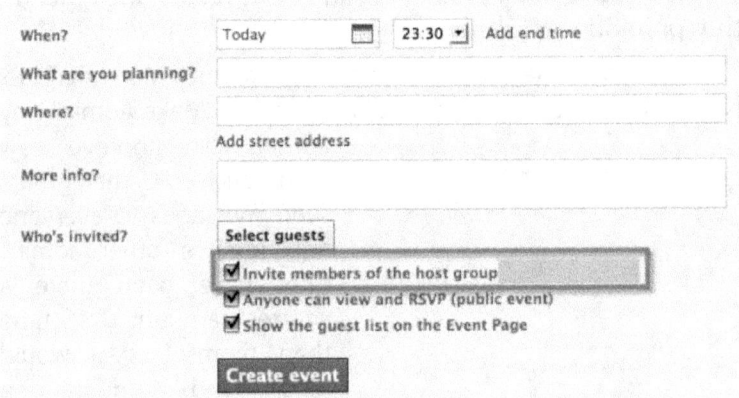

Note: For larger events where the guests don't necessarily know each other, it's sometimes best to hide the guest list for the privacy of your guests.

There are several things you should always do when creating events:

- Set the time, date, place and event name (make sure these are correct before you invite people!)
- Set how public your event is.
- Add extra details, like telling people what to bring or adding a picture.
- Invite people.
  - Remember your privacy – Don't add anyone's personal details (addresses or phone numbers) to a public event.

Facebook Pages

Facebook Pages are specific pages designed for business, brands, products, high-profile individuals, bands, websites and other things people may "like". If you manage one of these entities, it is recommended to create a Facebook Page in order to connect with your fans.

If someone has already created a Facebook Page for your product, don't be too worried. It's likely that it was created by a genuine fan who wanted to help promote your cause – they've probably done you many favours in your absence. It is also possible to prove to Facebook that you are the legal representative so that you can continue the work from there. Other things you may consider is discussing shared ownership with the current owner, leaving their page as an unofficial version or asking Facebook to delete their page entirely. Obviously, some of these options will endear yourself to your fans more than others; think about it diplomatically.

As mentioned before, the creator of the fan page will normally be an individual logged in with their own Facebook identity. Ensure this person is a reliable, stable member of your organisation as they will ultimately control your Facebook Page.

Also ensure this person is presentable enough to be a public face for your company and that they understand basic public relations and technical needs. You may have to rely on them at times, so be very careful who you choose!

Social Networking

It is also possible to create a page with a business account. While you are not logged in to Facebook, go to Facebook Pages and create a page.

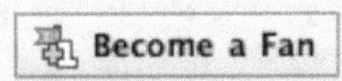

If you don't have your Facebook account click on "I do not have a Facebook account" and enter an email, password and date of birth. From there it will guide you through the steps to create a business account. Business accounts are not like other user accounts and cannot be used to view user profiles, make friends or be seen in search results. These accounts are simply for administration of Pages and Advertisements.

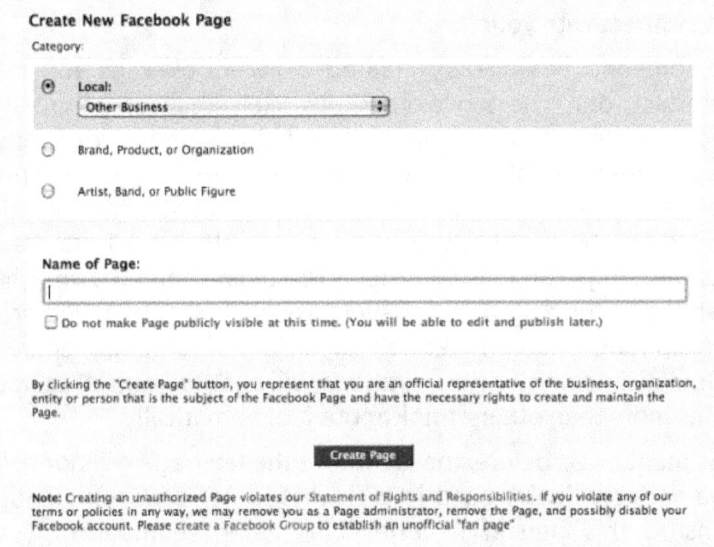

Ensure that whoever creates the Facebook Page adds multiple administrators as soon as possible, who are equally reliable, tech-savvy, presentable members of your organisation. This will save trouble in the future if the creator is unable to log in, make changes or moderate, if their account gets hacked or if they ever do decide to leave the organisation.

Also ensure your administrators are keeping their private life adequately private from prying eyes, as being an administrator will bring them into the public's scrutiny and firing line. This is to protect your staff as well as your reputation.

To add new administrators, edit the page, then click on "Manage Admins".

Once created there are many ways you can edit your Facebook Page to best represent your product. We'll go into tips and tricks later, but start yourself off by adding a few details you feel are essential for introductions, information and promotion.

Tip: When you've created your Page and are viewing it, click on "Bookmarks" and "Add Bookmark" in the navigation menu in order to add a quick bookmark to your page.

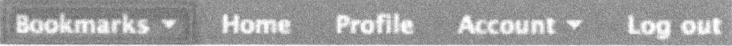

With new pages, you will automatically be notified when people comment on your page; you can opt for email notifications as well. Photos will be displayed at the top of your profile in the same way as user profiles.

As an administrator of a new Facebook Page, you'll be able to comment and "Like" other pages on behalf of your page. To do this, go to account on the navigation bar and choose "Use Facebook as Page".

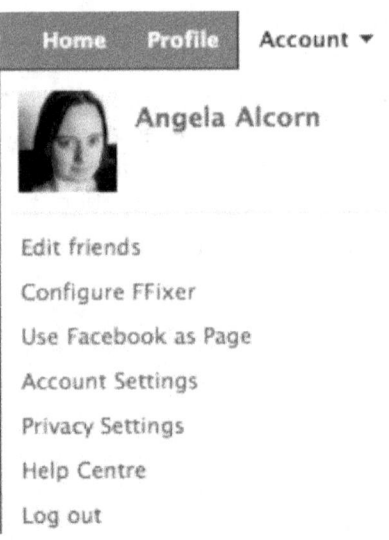

Facebook Page Insights

Facebook Page administrators can view the statistical insights of the page by visiting the Insights page. Here you'll find graphical representations of your Page's data, such as daily "Likes", interaction with posts, demographics and more. Insights can also be emailed to administrators on a weekly basis.

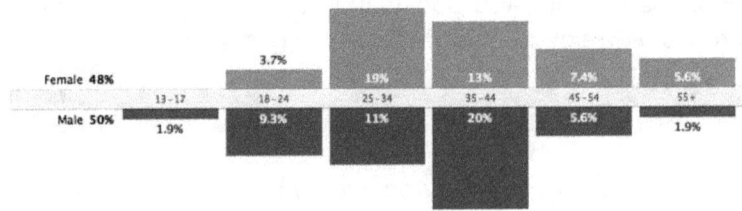

Keeping track of these statistics will enable you to make informed choices as to how popular certain posts were on Facebook, who is interested in your work and what to promote in the future.

Facebook Marketing Tools

Events for Pages

As a business, personality, brand or product, you might already have ideas as to what sort of events you will be promoting. If not, some typical ideas would include:

- Sales
- Openings/Launches
- Tours
- Signings & Celebrity Appearances
- Performances & Live Events
- VIP parties
- Virtual Events
- Causes & Fundraising Drives.

When viewing your Facebook Page, you'll notice you can't create an event from the status bar. You can't create an event from within the Page's edit page either (this used to be the way to do it). These days, you need to manage your Facebook event through an individual or a group. This is where it becomes very handy to have a staff group or volunteer group related to your page to create the event. Creating the event via a group also allows for a professional appearance and a kickstart at your event marketing, since you can invite all the group members immediately. See "Events for Groups" to create an event this way.

Facebook Community Pages

Facebook Community Pages are auto-generated using information from Wikipedia, Facebook Questions related to the topic and Facebook updates related to the page. They're usually based on towns, cities and regions.

To make the most of these pages, show your allegiance by "Liking" the page and

Add to my page's favourites
Unlike
Create a Page
Report Page
Share

adding it to your Page's favourites. Once you do this, your posts that mention the name of this page will appear in the "Related Posts" section, providing more exposure for you.

Facebook Networks

Facebook Networks used to be Facebook's way of grouping individuals by country, school or business. These days, networks can still be created for businesses and schools, but they don't hold the same meaning as they used to do. It can be an effective way of validating an individual as being an employee or student at a particular organisation, since Facebook ensures that an email address from that domain is verified for that account.

In regards to marketing, Networks don't hold a lot of power any more. It's best to use Groups, Pages and Places.

Applications

Facebook applications are incredibly viral and can be made to be quite effective. Creating a Facebook application is potentially a good marketing move, as long as you know why you're doing it and how it will aid your efforts.

Obviously writing an application from scratch is beyond the scope of this manual, but Facebook has developed a "Getting Started" guide for application developers. This is recommended as a first point of call.

Facebook Connect

Facebook Connect is a type of Facebook application, which is used to allow Facebook users to log into your website using their Facebook login. Anyone can set up Facebook Connect on their site, although many prefer to use Facebook Connect in conjunction with other login services, such as Disqus in order to allow people choices of Twitter and other logins as well. Others use Wordpress plugins to make the setup process easier.

There are also other important aspects to Facebook Connect which make it a valuable marketing tool. When your site uses Facebook Connect, any articles a reader likes on your site can be

Facebook Marketing Tools

displayed on their Facebook newsfeed, and those articles may be read by the user's friends.

Facebook Instant Personalisation

Some websites have partnered with Facebook to provide Instant Personalisation for their users. This personalisation means you'll also be able to show your readers on your site which posts their friends liked from your site, meaning they're more likely to pay attention to those posts before they leave your site. It's an easy way to increase engagement on your site and to boost the amount of time people spend on your site.

Advertising

Advertising on Facebook is an obvious marketing technique. Currently Facebook can offer exposure to up to 500 million people, targeted by specific demographics such as location, age and interest.

There are many options available to the advertiser, allowing budgets to be limited, the advertiser to specify whether to cost per click (CPC) or pay per view (PPV), users interests can be specified, and the location can be set to an extremely local area.

Due to this, Facebook advertising is a promising venture even to non-profit organisations such as theatre groups wanting to audition local actors for a specific role.

Reach your target customers
- Connect with more than 500 million potential customers
- Select your audience by location, age and interests
- Test simple image and text-based adverts and use what works

Deepen your relationships
- Promote your Facebook Page or website
- Use our "Like" button to increase the influence of your advert
- Build a community around your business

Control your budget
- Set the daily budget you are comfortable with
- Adjust your daily budget at any time
- Choose to pay only when people click (CPC) or see your advert (CPM)

Facebook Places

Facebook Places is Facebook's way of letting users "check in" to venues, letting their friends know where they're hanging out. It

Social Networking

improves the venue's exposure to that user's friends in the news feed, plus it breeds loyalty to the venue.

To control your business in Facebook Places, first check if it's already listed. Search for your business name in the search bar. If there is a place with your business name, you can claim it as your business by following the link labelled "Is this your business?" and following the claims process from there. You'll be verified by phone and can then edit your business' place details, such as opening hours and profile pictures.

If your business isn't listed in Facebook Places, you can add it yourself. You'll need to use a supported device, log into the Facebook application and open Facebook Places while in your business physically so the location is correctly set. Click on "Check in" then "Add" and fill out the name details as you wish. Finish by going back to "Check in". Once the place is in the system, follow the previous instructions to claim it as your business.

Places
Who. What. When. And now **Where**.

Share where you are	Connect with friends nearby	New: Find local deals

"Best. Concert. Ever."	"I'm just down the street!"	I'm getting £20 off new jeans.
Easily share where you are, what you're doing and the friends you're with right from your mobile.	Never miss another chance to connect when you happen to be in the same place at the same time.	Check in to get individual discounts, share savings with friends, earn rewards for repeat visits or secure donations for good causes.
• Check in and your update will appear on the Place page, your friends' News Feeds and your Wall.	• Browse status updates of friends checked in nearby.	• Use Facebook Places on your mobile to find special offers everywhere — just look for the deal logo.
• Tag the friends you're with so they can be part of your update.	• After checking in, tap "Here now" to see who else is checked in where you are.	• Save at your favourite retailers, eateries and entertainment venues too.
• Appear in "Here now" to friends and others nearby who are also checked in.		• Check in to claim a deal and let friends know about it.

Once you have set up a Facebook Place for your business, there are numerous ways you might engender loyalty and engagement with your venue, such as offering discounts for people who check in and discounts for loyalty. These deals are then passed on to friends via the newsfeed, possibly encouraging more people to take part in your deal later. That's some quick word of mouth publicity!

Merging Facebook Places and Pages

It's possible to merge your Facebook Places location with your Facebook Page, however this is not always recommended. For small businesses with specific pages, this is okay, but you wouldn't want to merge a specific franchise location with a global brand. Also, some functionality is removed after the merge, such as being able to choose which tab is the landing page for the Facebook Page. Any Facebook users connected with the page or place will be connected to the new merged page.

Overall, though many people believe merging Places and Pages to be a good thing for branding, administration and simplicity. If you want to merge your place and page, visit the place you have claimed in Facebook and click on the "Merge this place with a page" link. Facebook staff will verify that this is indeed a matching place and page, and then merge them for you. The merge process cannot be reversed.

Tips & Tricks

There are numerous ways to make your business shine on Facebook. Using the right mix of Facebook products and a few tried and tested marketing tactics, you'll be doing quite well. But sometimes it's worth knowing how Facebook works, who uses Facebook, what works specifically on Facebook (plus what doesn't) and how you might do better.

So, here are some great ideas for marketing yourself on Facebook. Don't get trapped in Facebook. One of the most important things to remember about Facebook is that information you put directly into Facebook is essentially stuck in Facebook. So, if you don't want your company to become dependent on Facebook, don't create your best content in Facebook. Instead, create content elsewhere (like your blog) and link to it from Facebook. Some people even go so far as to sync Twitter updates as Facebook updates so that the content is also in the wider Internet. Whatever you do is entirely your choice, but it's always worth bearing in mind.

Social Networking

Facebook is huge right now, but no one knows what the future holds. If you keep Facebook as a part of your marketing effort, rather than the entirety of your efforts, you're in a good position for the future.

Create Engaging Content

As for blogs, Facebook Pages should provide regular engaging content (which is not too controversial). Ask questions, tell stories – whatever you do, stay interesting! Don't make it sound like an advert and don't bore your fans. Offer tips and tricks, mention relevant news and try to encourage comments and feedback.

Sharing links on a page

The quickest and most effective way to engage your audience is to share links to great content, asking for comments and opinions from your fans. Make sure you also use the best thumbnail to get their attention.

To do this, head to your Page's status bar, click on "Link" and paste the URL in. You also use the same process to share photos, video, questions and status updates.

Don't Post Too Often

Some users will un-like a Facebook Page if their posts take over their home feed. How you determine how many posts is enough or too much is up to you, but most people consider once per week to once per day as sufficient.

Make Your Facebook Page Interesting

Not only do photos make a brand seem more trustworthy, they also add colour. The easiest way to brighten up your Facebook Page is with a large vertical banner as a profile picture. Currently the size limit is 180x540px. This will take up the entire left-hand panel and bring more colour to your page.

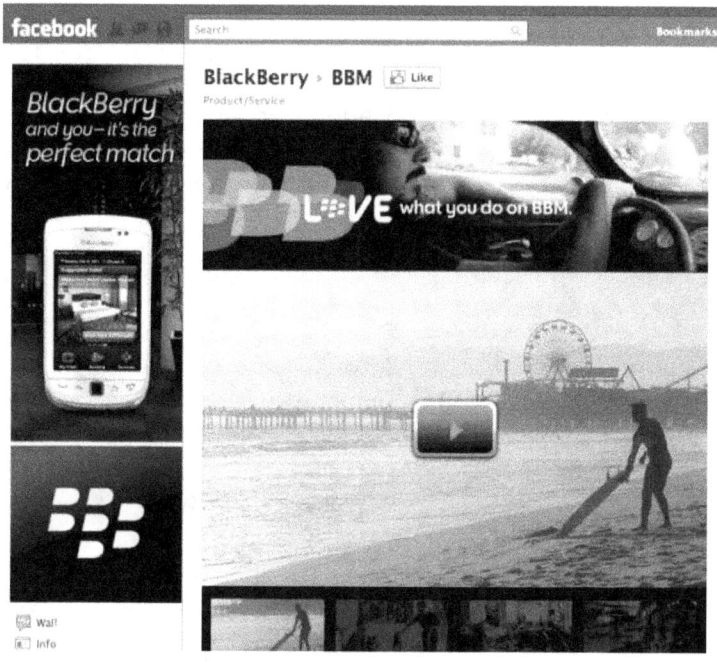

It's also possible to create a splash page with plenty of colour by setting a specific landing tab. You can even control these landing pages so that first-time visitors will see a different page to return visitors. This means you can give more of an overview to your potential audience, while getting straight into the gossip with your fans.

If you're not sure what to do with your welcome tab, search the Internet for "best Facebook pages" and you will find many great blog posts with more examples of innovative Facebook Pages.

The easiest way to set up a welcome tab for your page is to add an application todo this. Go to "Edit Page" then choose "Apps". At the bottom of the page, there should be a suggested application called Static FBML (or use the given link). Add the application and it will allow you to write your own HTML for that tab, allowing pictures, video and other interactive features to be used. Click on "Go To Application" to add the HTML to the tab.

Social Networking

Static FBML
Add advanced functionality to your Page using the Facebook Static FBML application. This application will add a box to your Page in which you can render HTML or FBML (Facebook Markup Language) for enhanced Page customisation.
Go to application · Edit settings

To change your default landing tab, visit your page's wall and click on "Edit Page" and "Manage Permissions". Click on the options for "Default landing tab for everyone else" and choose the FBML tab.

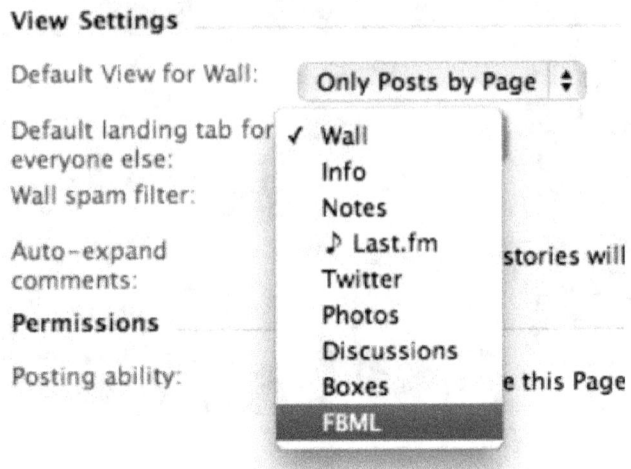

Another option to create a landing tab is to use Pagemodo (also here).

One of the best tricks used in these landing page designs is to use a little bit of space at the top to reminder users to "Like" the page while they're there.

Also use your landing page to tell your readers exactly what sort of tips and tricks they'll learn by "Liking" your page and following your updates. Not only will they know exactly what they're signing up for and why they'll look forward to learning more and will really pay attention to your posts.

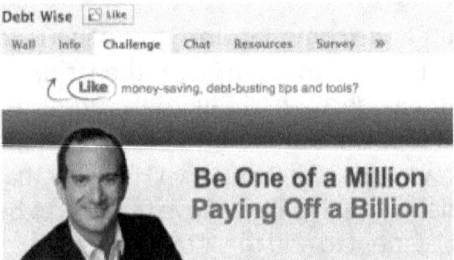

Also, be creative with the new page design. Now that pages have photo thumbnails across the top like the new profile pages, you can use all the same profile design tricks available to personal profiles to make your wall more interesting. Give it a go!

Importing Blog entries to Page notes: Although Facebook links are paid more attention than Facebook Notes, notes can be an easy way of managing updates to a Facebook Profile.

To do this, go to your page's notes tab and import the RSS feed for your blog. Also, make sure in your wall settings that you allow auto-expanding of comments so that thumbnails of blog pictures will be included in the update on your wall.

This trick is great for people who just want to set up a profile and forget it. It won't lead to true engagement, but it's far better than having a stagnant page.

Facebook Page Applications

Use Facebook Page applications to incorporate other social media efforts, such as your content from Flickr, YouTube, Tumblr, Slideshare and Twitter. Why waste all your effort duplicating content when you could be making more use of it? Also, Non-Profits should consider using causes to help their campaigns.

Go to "Edit Page" and "Apps" to see your current applications and to find new ones.

Facebook Questions

Facebook Questions is something you've probably seen as a regular Facebook user, but it's worth using as a marketing tool for brands and personalities on Facebook. Consider occasionally using Facebook for a conversation about which pool cleaning products people use and why they choose them. You could also try polling and quizzes from other applications.

Mentions of Groups / Events / Pages

Encourage and perhaps educate your fans to mention your Page, Event and Groups in their status updates. For users to do this while entering a status update, they just need to enter @ and follow it with the first letters of your page/event/group's name until they can click on your name. This is an easy way for them to let all of their friends know about your promotions as your Page ("Accounts" then "Use Facebook as Page"), then searching through Questions to answer queries for people. You'll be adding value for your customers, building awareness of your brand and helping people to understand your areas of expertise.

Also consider asking good questions or starting polls to help bring up conversations about things related to your brand.

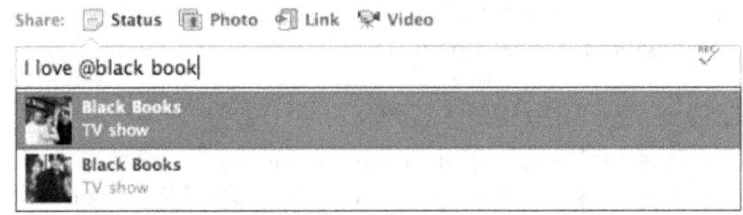

Give-aways & Contests

Give things away and hold contests. Yes, it's true – the things that work for real-life marketing can also work within Facebook. Just make sure you stick within Facebook guidelines when promoting contests.

Asking your fans to vote on something is another great way to build engagement and to encourage your fans to share your page with their friends.

Love UK has done a great job of this, using Places and a custom application to incorporate a leader board of the best destinations in the UK into their page. Plus, their application lets users see which of their friends have been to these places, leading to more user interaction and the potential for more future trips to these destinations.

Facebook Marketing Tools

Promote Your Facebook Presence Offline & Elsewhere Online

Use real-life signage and business cards to promote your Facebook Page, Place, events and online competitions. Keep the word spreading from online to offline andback again. The same goes for your blog and other online profiles. Make sure your Facebook Page, Events, Places and photos are featured in a blog post, in the sidebar and in other profiles such as your Flickr or YouTube profile.

Facebook offers many different styles of widget for your websites, from script-based to image-based, so you will be able to find something to use.

Go to "Edit Settings" on your page and click "Marketing" then "Get a Badge" or "Get a like box for your website".

From here, you can also make an advert for your Facebook page. Be sure to include a 'like' button (this one is recommended by Facebook advertising).

There are many ways to promote your Page
- Advertise on Facebook
- Tell your fans
- Get a badge
- Add a Like Box to your website
- Create alias
- Send an update

Have Goals

As with all marketing efforts, it's good to set some quantifiable goals for your Facebook strategy. How many "Likes" do you want? By when? How many

Social Networking

people would you like commenting per week? How much traffic would you like Facebook to send to your website?

Or do you want to focus on customer service oriented goals: How many customers have you helped? How have you built community around your brand?

Once you know your goals, you can create a strategy to achieve them. You may need to ensure regular updates from several staff members in order to maintain your page's momentum.

Moderation

If you allow comments or photo uploads, you will need someone (or several people) to moderate your Facebook Page for abuse and offensive comments. To ensure the best possible interactions with your fans, try to make very clear what sorts of posts are encouraged and discouraged, so that everyone knows what will be removed and what will be kept.

The new Facebook Pages make moderation even easier, allowing you to create a blocklist of keywords to automatically filter out. You can even automatically block profanity using a drop down filter option. Go to "Edit Settings" and "Manage Permissions".

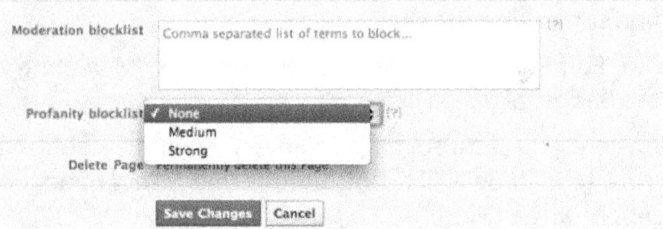

Be Authentic

Ensure your brand stays true to its roots. Don't try to be something you're not on Facebook. Also add a human touch, by allowing your staff to converse a little with your fans. If your staff can sign-on with their own name after they post on behalf of the company, it will also help to show the real personalities behind the brand.

Thank Your Fans

Don't take your fans for granted. Offer discounts or some sort of reward if possible. At the very least, thank them for their support.

Engage and Facilitate Conversation

If your fans are leaving comments (good or bad), make sure someone is on hand to respond to these. Deal with PR and customer service issues immediately, and continue to encourage conversation.

Facilitate communication between your following by allowing your fans to upload photos or ask questions to other fans.

Conclusion

Marketing on Facebook is something that will change rapidly and without warning. Basic marketing principles can often be used within Facebook, but your best value will be gained by generally focusing on engagement, conversation, good customer service, offering valuable information, providing shareable media, bright visuals and not being overly sales-focused with your content.

Syncing Facebook with Twitter and other Social Media

If you or your organisation has profiles across several social media sites (such as Twitter) you may want to consider synching the accounts. If you are new to Twitter or not on the service yet, see the other chapters. Synching the accounts means that whenever you update one account, the other will automatically update to reflect whatever you wrote. For example, say you change your Facebook status, if your account is linked with a Twitter account, you will automatically tweet your recently updated status. This can save your time, and keep all of your social media sites up to date. Facebook and Twitter can be linked directly through your Facebook. To link your Facebook to your Twitter account, you will need to add the Social Tweet application. To do this, simply "Social Tweet" into your search box at the top of your page. You should see the results below:

Social Networking

Clicking the Application button will bring up the following box:

Follow the prompts to set up your account and you will be tweeting updates in no time!

If you have multiple social accounts (such as Twitter, Facebook & LinkedIn) you may want to consider a service that will update all accounts, the easiest way to do this is to sign up for a free account on a third party site that will sync all accounts.

A great site to check out is Ping.fm. All you have to do is sign up for an account on Ping.fm, and then register all of the information for all of your social outlets.

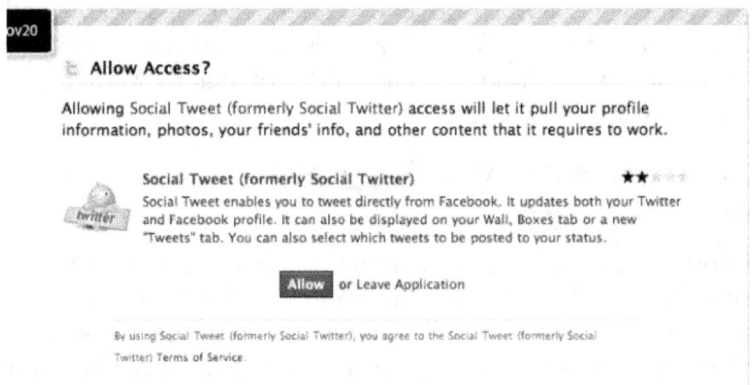

Now whenever you update one, all of your other pages will update as well.

Remember, social media is about being social. Updating all with the same info will detract from your appeal on each service.

Deactivating Your Account

There may come a time when you want to delete your Facebook account. To do this, simply follow the steps outlined below:

- ★ Click the Settings tab
- ★ Click Deactivate in the Deactive Account Section
- ★ The Confirm Facebook Deactivation screen is displayed
- ★ Select the reason you are deactivating your Facebook account
- ★ Enter the security code displayed in the box in the Text in the Box field
- ★ Click the Deactivate button
- ★ Now that you know what all you can do with Facebook, the trick is to not become overwhelmed by trying to do everything at once. Start slow by sending friend requests to your friends and family and reading what's up on their wall. Once you get accustomed to the service, you can expand your use to uploading photo albums, and from there, begin experimenting with some of the neat Facebook applications, creating a Page, and a whole lot more!

Tipoff
That's all about Facebook. Now you must have made presence on Internet, and your engines must be producing tons of money!!! Let us now open an online store on Ebay!

Do affiliate Marketing on Facebook and earn extra income to your Money Plant.

Chapter 9

E-Mail Marketing & Newsletters

As you have setup everything, now you need something to tell your customers about what are your future plans and what progress your Brand/Blog/Website has made.

Do it by E-mail Marketing Campaigns. Send your Newsletters containing all information regarding progress and future plan to your customers. Since you are using Electronic Newsletter, do some **Affiliate Marketing** here, post ads and links of your partners here; means double benefits. First you expand your business through these Newsletters and second you get credit from ads posted.

Information on E-mail Marketing & Newsletters

Email marketing has been a staple for consumer marketers since the mid-90s. A few years later, B2B marketers discovered its value, and email campaigns have become an important tool for businesses in all stages and industries.

Email marketing enables you to cost-effectively communicate with your market in a way that's immediate and relevant. With email, you can:

- ☆ Nurture leads
- ☆ Build brand awareness
- ☆ Obtain prospects
- ☆ Build customer loyalty
- ☆ Generate sales

You can usually launch a campaign and measure your results fairly quickly, making email a great option for time-sensitive programs. It's easy and inexpensive to test different aspects of your campaign on a segment of your list, so you can hone your creative and your offer to generate the best possible results.

Email is more editorial than advertising, and it's powerful because it can support and even drive a sales process. Yet like any medium, it has its challenges. Business people get hundreds of emails (or more) each day, so you'll need to get your message past spam filters and give them a reason to read. You'll also need a strong offer, valuable editorial content, appropriate design and a good fulfillment and measurement process.

You can reach a wide audience with email, but that doesn't mean you should. It's most effective when you really target, so you can speak to specific needs. Think of it as a one-to-one communication – personalised, relevant, timely – not a blast.

Before you begin

Use email to meet the goals you set in your annual **marketing plan**; you can also use them as part of a broader **marketing campaign**. You'll also need to make sure your **website** is strong enough to support your campaign.

Develop your campaign around specific goals

Take the time to strategise and plan your campaign:

- ☆ Develop a tangible objective – for example, to generate a specific number of leads, demo requests, meetings, or purchases.
- ☆ Profile and target your audience. You can reach a large audience through email, but that doesn't mean.
- ☆ you should narrow targeting, means you can speak more directly to their needs.
- ☆ Create a good offer and compelling call-to-action, and present it early in your message – readers skim.

- ✯ Plan a series of emails to create an ongoing campaign – it takes multiple touches to generate response.
- ✯ Don't forget fulfillment – if your prospects expect a phone call or email, deliver it quickly or you could lose their interest.

Invest in good content

Few people want to read emails that look and feel like ads. Instead, offer information that's relevant to your recipients. It's an investment to develop that content, but it's the content that gets people to open your messages and continue to read them over time.

Choose the right technology

If you've never launched an email campaign, you'll probably need to use an email service provider (ESP), typically a web-based service. Choose a reputable ESP to help you stay compliant with spam legislation and get your messages to your prospects' inboxes – a major issue in email marketing. A good ESP can raise your delivery rate, manage your opt-in and opt-out process, keep your email list clean and provide reports that can help you improve your results.

Be respectful and follow industry practices

- ✯ Make sure you're following accepted industry practices – you'll improve your probability of success.
- ✯ Mail to your house list regularly – even corporate emails change rapidly. The more time between campaigns, the higher your rate of bad addresses – and those "bounces" could trigger spam alerts.
- ✯ Make sure your recipients can easily opt-out of future communications.
- ✯ If you're buying or renting a list, make sure it's an "opt-in" list.

Continually Test, Refine and Improve

It's always wise to test before launching a campaign. If you're working with a new ESP or list, evaluate your delivery and response rate before you roll out. Keep testing and improving your subject lines, headlines and copy, design, offer, landing pages, even the delivery timing. You'll improve all your campaigns in the process.

What's next?

As email becomes more important in your overall strategy, keep learning about the subject and improving your campaigns.

Chapter 10

Online Scam, Identity Theft & Prevention

Please Beware of following on Internet:
1. Never reply to unsolicited Mails
2. Never give your Details including you Bio-data to anyone.
3. Sometimes you get messages for reviewing your Credit and Debit Cards, Never Share this information.
4. If you are shopping online, check for SSL and VeriSign Verification pages before checking out.
5. Never reply to unknown messages
6. You will never get anything "free" on internet, so please try to mind it. Yes you may go for some freebies (But those are samples only)
7. In any way never share your information with any third party
8. Always work under secure environment, use standard search engines, never install toolbars, they sometime monitor your online behaviour
9. Always install a good anti-malware on your system
10. Take care of your personal data honestly.
11. Contact your ISP for better environment, block your stolen data immediately in the case of any identity theft.

Example of Famous Scams in India (You mostly get this on by SMS and E-mail)

Example 1:

Mail saying you have won billions!

---Attached---

From: Shellpriceaward@centrum.cz
<Shellpriceaward@centrum.cz>

Subject: CONGRATS! YOU WON 200,000.00 GREAT BRITAIN POUNDS!

TO:

DATE: THURSDAY, JUNE 11 2011

Shell Petroleum Development Company Of England
Shell center, London, SE1 7NA- United Kingdom

BATCH REF: 88888/OI

This is to inform you that you have won a prize of 200,000.00 GB Pounds) for the June 2011 International E-mail draw organised by SPDC.

SPDC collects all the email addresses of the people that are active online, among millions that subscribed to Yahoo, Aol, Walla, Gmail, Russian Mail and Hotmail.

Six people are selected Monthly to benefit from this promotion and you are one of the selected winners.

PAYMENT OF PRIZE AND CLAIM

Winners shall be paid in accordance with his/her settlement center. Shell award must be claimed not later than 15 days from the Date of Draw Notification. Any Prize not claimed within this period will be forfeited.

Stated below is your identification number-

Online Scam, Identity Theft & Prevention

REFERNCE NUMBER: SPDC-77411

Contact Mr. Tam David West with your contact details and a sum of RS. 25000 (It will be required to process your Order)

E-Mail: mrtdwest@yahoo.com

Tel: +234 803 082 0739

Congratulations! Once again!

Yours in Service,

Dr.(Mr.)Johnson Brown

[Publicity Secretory]

Example 2:

Mail saying they need your details,

Mr. XYZ,

We are customer care from ABC Bank. Your Account has been hacked by some online hackers, and we need your credit card, debit card & net-banking details. It's urgent or you will be charged Rs. 100000 for they are going to hack and transfer your money.

Thanking you

Mr. DEF

Chief Phishing Controller

ABC Bank

<u>Advice: Never ever disclose your information; your bank never need these details!</u>

Phishing Website Methods

The fraudulent website that supports the phishing email is designed to mirror the legitimate website it is purporting to be. The fraudsters use multiple methods to do this, including using genuine looking images and text, disguising the URL in the address bar or removing the address bar altogether. The purpose of the website is to trick consumers into thinking they are at the company's genuine website, and giving their personal information to the trusted company they think they are dealing with.

1. Genuine Looking Content

Phishing websites utilise copied images, text and in some cases simply mirror the legitimate website. This will contain the normal links on the website such as contact us, privacy, products, services etc. The user recognises the website content from the genuine site and are unaware they are not on the genuine website.

2. Similar looking URL to Genuine URL

Some phishing websites have registered a domain name similar to that of the organisation they are appearing to be from. For example, one phishing scam we received targeting Barclays Bank used the domain name "http://www.barclayze.co.uk". Other examples include using a sub-domain such as "http://www.barclays.validation.co.uk", where the actual domain is "validation.co.uk" which is not related to Barclays Bank.

3. Form – Collection of Information

The most common method used to collect information in phishing scams is by the use of forms on the fake website. The form is normally displayed in the same format as that used on the genuine website. This may be an Internet Banking log-in, or a more detailed form for verification of personal details, with many fields for personally sensitive information.

4. Incorrect URL, not disguised

Some phishing scam websites do not even attempt to deceive users with their URL, and hope that the user does not notice.

Some simply use I.P Addresses displayed as numbers in the users address bar.

5. URL Spoofing of Address Bar (Fake)

This form of URL spoofing involves the removal of the address bar combined with the use of scripts to build a fake address bar using images and text. The link in the phishing email opens a new browser window, which closes and re-opens without the address bar, and in some case the status bar. The new window uses HTML, HTA and JavaScript commands to construct a false address bar in place of the original. (See figure 1 below)

As this method utilises scripts, it is only possible to stop this form of deception by disabling active x and JavaScript in browser settings. As most webpages utilise these normal tools, this is impractical.

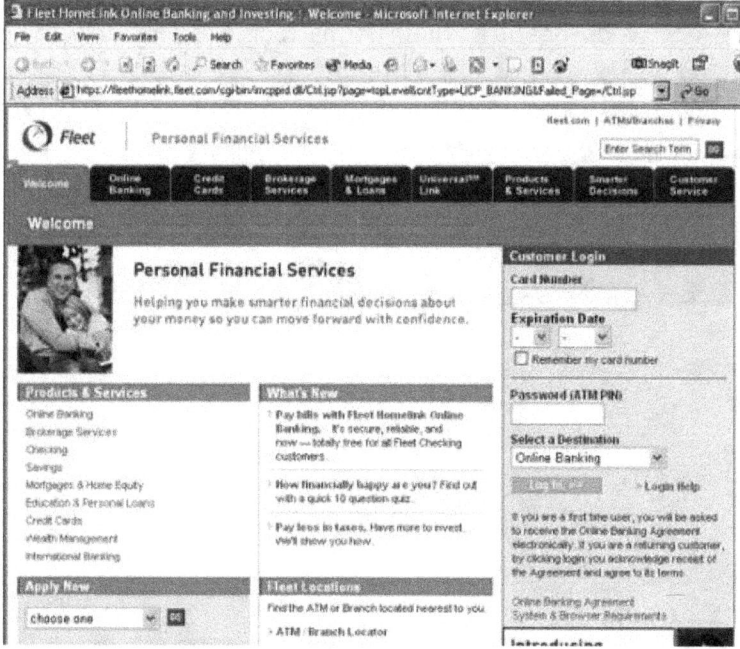

Figure 1. Fake Address Bar displayed. Notice the change in colour on the right? You can also observe if you click on the drop down arrow on the address bar, the history is empty.

Social Networking

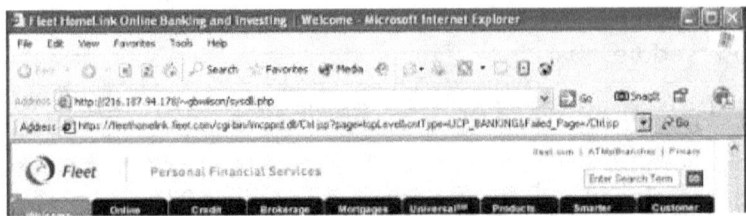

Figure 2. *A closer look. Right click on a toolbar, tick address bar. This shows the correct address bar with the correct URL.*

6. Hovering Text Box over Address Bar

This form of URL spoofing involves the placement of a text object with a white background over the URL in the address bar. The text object contains the fake URL, which covers the genuine URL.

As this method utilises scripts, it is only possible to stop this form of deception by disabling Active X and JavaScript in browser settings. As most webpages utilise these normal tools, this is impractical.

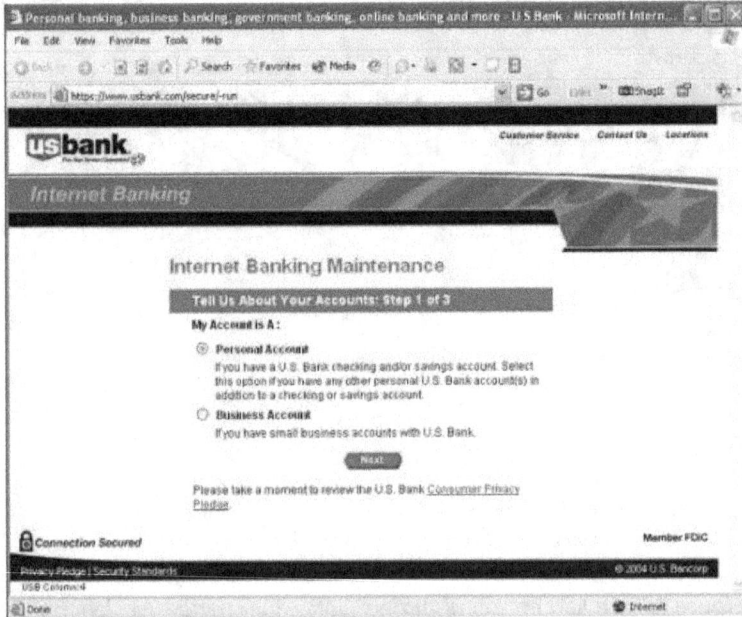

Figure 3. *Fake Address Bar displayed using a hovering text box. Virtually impossible to pick when glancing at the address bar.*

Online Scam, Identity Theft & Prevention

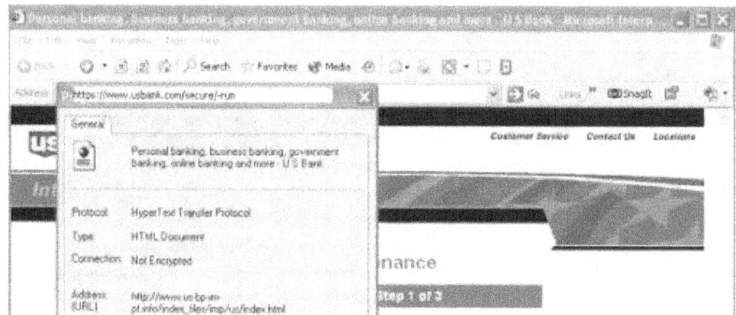

Figure 4. *A closer look. Select properties from the File menu. The properties box shows us the correct URL, whilst also highlighting the white text box hovering over the address bar.*

7. Pop Up Windows

This form of deception involves the use of script to open a genuine webpage in the background while a bare pop up window (without address bar, tool bars, status bar and scrollbars) is opened in the foreground to display the fake webpage, in an attempt to mislead the user to think it is directly associated to the genuine page. (See figure 6 below)

As this method utilises scripts, it is only possible to stop this form of deception by disabling Active X and JavaScript in browser settings. As most webpages utilise these normal tools, this is impractical.

Social Networking

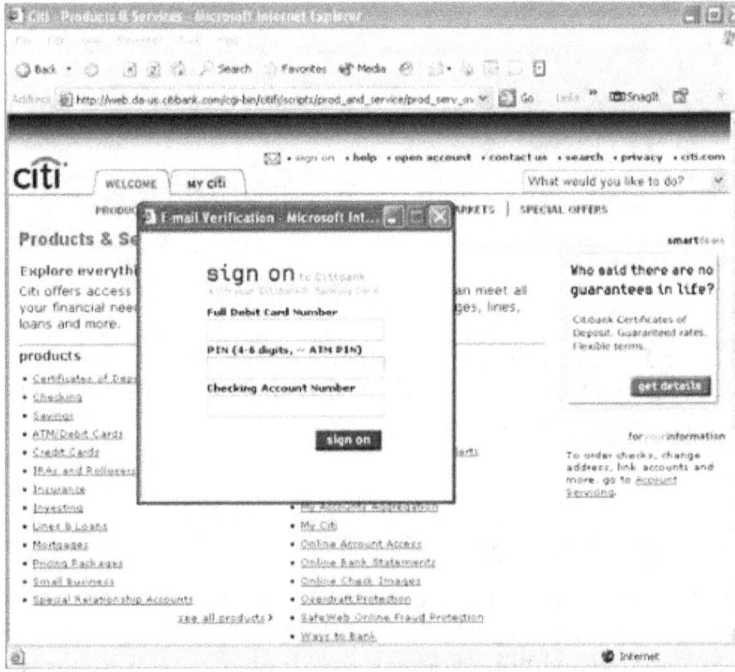

Figure 5. *Genuine Citibank webpage is displayed in the background, while the fake webpage is displayed in a pop up window in the foreground.*

8. Trojans / Spyware

Trojan and worm viruses are sent to the user as an email attachment, purporting to be for some type of purpose, such as greetings, important files or other type of SPAM email. The attachment is a program that exploits vulnerabilities in Internet Browsing software to force a download from another computer on the Internet. This file downloads other files and codes, which eventually installs a fully functional Trojan virus.

The Trojan is designed to harvest, or search for personal banking information and passwords, which many people keep on their computer. This information is then sent to a remote computer on the Internet.

Other worms have been known to hijack the user's HOST file, which causes an automatic redirection to a fake phishing website when the user types in a specific URL (normally for a specific financial institution) into the address bar of their Internet browser.

Spyware, such as keyboard loggers, capture information entered at legitimate websites, such as Internet banking sites. This type of spyware can be planted on a user's computer using a previous worm or Trojan infection. Any information the spyware captures is sent to a predetermined computer on the Internet.

A recent phishing scam used the link in the email to direct the users browsers to a site to first download keyboard logging spyware before redirecting the user to the genuine Internet banking website. This spyware captured the login information entered, and sent this information to the fraudsters via a remote computer on the Internet.

Estimated that each year $10 million is lost by Indians in these spams, so beware next time!!!

Protect Yourself!

Hey! You are here! If you read this book thoroughly and followed it strictly than you will find yourself earning Rs.27398.... Now you are going to be Millionaire?

Help your friends, relatives and dear ones to become Millionaire by simply encouraging them to buy this book.

Author: Prof. Shrikant Prasoon
Format: Paperback
Language: English
Pages: 248
Price: ₹ 175.00

Author: Anchit Barnwal
Format: Paperback
Language: English
Pages: 168
Price: ₹ 200.00

Author: Shikha Gupta & Shikha Nautiyal
Format: Paperback
Language: English
Pages: 104
Price: ₹ 100.00

Chanakya was both a destructive and creative thinker able to annihilate an established empire and erect and establish another larger, richer and greater on the debris, without money, material and man. So, he is the only qualified person in human history to be Guru; Acharya; Teacher; Guide and Mentor in the field of Management. With his super mind and supreme determination he succeeded in everything and everywhere; and wrote down everything without inhibitions or secrecy for the posterity in his three monumental works:

1. Teachings of Kautilya's Arthashastra & Nitishastra
2. Perfect Analogy between Ancient Managerial System & Modern Corporate Setup

Just as a winning podium can accommodate anyone on it, each one of us is capable to be a winner, irrespective of our shortcomings and differences. Winners' Podium – Everyone Fits on it, attempts to do just that: make out a winner amongst each one of us.

This book offers elaborate guidelines for a balanced, successful and happy living. It tells how one can find his talent, attract ideas and be successful, both personally and professionally. It also talks of happiness and the steps to it.

Through stories, anecdotes, quotations, examples and day to day observations, this book can inspire you to not only attain that most desirable success, but also to hold on and grow both internally and externally with it.

Introduction to Computers is an effort made with an interactive and hands on approach to communicate the essential aspects of computers. The book targets children of all ages. Interesting fun characters make the learning a fun process for readers.

Features of the Book:

Assessment Exercises: Each unit of the book contains interesting lesson-end assessment exercise to assess and examine your understanding and grasp over the subject.

Computer Trivia: This part of the book gives an interesting outlook of the vast computer world and some factual knowledge regarding computers.

Did you know: This portion provides information related to historical aspects of computer world. Developmental features of computers are also highlighted.

visit our online bookstore: **www.vspublishers.com**

www.ingramcontent.com/pod-product-compliance
Lightning Source LLC
Chambersburg PA
CBHW070335230426
43663CB00011B/2327